PENTATONIC

TEACH LIKE IT'S
MUSIC

AN ARTFUL APPROACH TO EDUCATION

DOUG GOODKIN

WITH ILLUSTRATIONS BY ELI NOYES

"Character is the backbone of our human culture and music is the flowering of character. When music prevails and the people's mind are led toward the right ideals and aspirations, we may see the appearance of a great nation."

—CONFUCIUS (551–479 BC)

"Without music the state cannot exist. All the disorders, all the wars we behold through the world occur only because of the neglect to learn music…"

—MOLIERE (1622–1673)

"People who make music together can't be enemies, at least while the music lasts."

—PAUL HINDEMITH (1895–1963)

"To a humanity looking for elements of hope, music ought to be an important matter. We may even say that man will begin to recover the moment he takes art as seriously as physics, chemistry or money. There is no other human activity that asks for such a harmonious cooperation of 'intellect' and 'soul' as artistic creation and, especially, music.…To destructive analysis music opposes synthesis, to the uniformization of science, which reduces qualities to quantities, music opposes a hierarchy of values. Our mechanized minds need to be musicalized…"

—ERNST LEVY (1895–1981)

"For rhythm and harmony penetrate deeply into the mind and take a most powerful hold on it, and if education is good, bring and impart grace and beauty."

—PLATO (c.427–347 B.C.)

"One thing he discovered with a great deal of astonishment was the music held more for him than just pleasure. There was meat to it. The grouping of sounds, their forms in the air as they rang out and faded, said something comforting to him about the rule of creation. What the music said was that there is a right way for things to be ordered so that life might not always be just tangle and drift, but have a shape, an aim. It was a powerful argument against the notion that things just happen."

—CHARLES FRAZIER (from his book *Cold Mountain*)

For further information, go to: www.douggoodkin.com

Cover Design: Lisa Berman
Cover Artwork: Augusta Talbot
Editors: Peter Greenwood/Kim McClain
Copy Editor: Kim McClain
Book design and typesetting: Bill Holab Music
ISBN 0-9773712-6-3

CONTENTS

PREFACE

This book, my ninth, has perhaps been the most difficult of all to write. Here I try to gather between two covers all the pedagogical scaffolding I talk about in my workshops and courses with teachers. In Orff workshops, teachers actively participate and then walk out the door with great new music, activities and lesson plans to try with their students. Yet without a clear understanding of the pedagogical ideas behind the activities, simply copying activities falls short. The best workshops include deep reflection on what we've done, how we've done it, why we've done it and what else we might do.

How to communicate these ideas without having the shared experience? In the workshop, these thoughts come after a series of activities and always make concrete reference to a lesson we have just done. How to engage the reader without the lesson first? That has been the difficult challenge, trying to draw the reader in with words alone. If I have failed, it is not through lack of effort. I believe I made at least eight drafts of every chapter and lost sleep looking for the perfect word or sentence, which didn't always arrive (but thankfully, sometimes did).

Much thanks in this regard goes to my primary editor Peter Greenwood, who kept insisting that a lean, mean prose would communicate better than my long-listed Whitmanesque style. Sometimes he gave up and let me have my way, but where the text sings better because of less clutter, I have him to thank. Jumping in on the pedagogical side was my Orff colleague Kim McClain and I thank her for her clarifying insights and suggestions, her affirmations of "I love this sentence!" and her meticulous copy-editing. My wife Karen, daughter Talia and colleague Sofía López-Ibor all read through some early drafts and made many helpful comments that helped shape a better book.

Given our image-soaked culture and wanting to lighten up the text with some playful drawings, I called upon Eli Noyes, illustrator of James Harding's book *From Wibbleton to Wobbleton* to keep these Pentatonic Press offerings consistent and recognizable. It's no easy task to render abstract thought into concrete images and after many spirited conversations, Eli did it masterfully. Since this book relates to my previous publication *The ABC's of Education*, it made perfect sense for Augusta Talbot who did that cover to do this one as well. Thanks to her for that fine work.

Gratitude yet again to Bill Holab for his always perfect layout work, Lisa Berman for cover layout, and all the Orff vendors who continue to carry my books. "It takes a village" to publish a book and this has been a most delightful community.

Finally, my sincere hopes that these ideas enter music classrooms worldwide and help make children's days a bit happier having enjoyed a music class taught musically. At the far end of a 45-year career teaching children and adults, I hope that revealing the details behind my practice helps pass the baton to the next generation. I am far from finished, but it is clear that the years behind far outnumber the years ahead. If this book can help light the way for those that follow, the struggle to put it all together will be well worth the effort.

Enjoy!

INTRODUCTION

"Suppose we set up in schools the same social improvements
that we are so proud of achieving? Let us feed the children,
give them playgrounds, clothing, freedom of speech… These
small things will be a beginning, but will not suffice and to
learn what greater remedies are needed, we must study the
nature of humanity as revealed in the first years of life. Then
we shall know with certainty what is needed." [*]

—MARIA MONTESSORI

What is the nature of the child? How does the mind work? What is
the role of the heart in learning? Good teaching begins with good
questions and then the long patient search for answers that make
children happy. Might we start to organize education around the
actual needs of children, start to plan our classes around the kinds of
experiences that motivate and inspire, affirm and challenge real kids?
To be a great teacher starts with a great story about who we are and
what we yet might become, a story born from patient observation
of children's nature and an unshakeable allegiance to the child still
within us as adults. Once our feet are planted firmly on that solid
ground, we're ready to consider how to proceed, guided in the day-
to-day by the north star of what makes children happy, what gives
them what they deeply need.

This book is based on three simple premises:

---

[*] Montessori, Maria: *To Educate the Human Potential;* Clio Press, 1989, p. 83

1. To educate effectively, we need to understand how the human mind—and body and heart and spirit— work. Once we understand, we then wrap all decisions and lesson plans and school culture around those understandings.

2. The brain is primed for survival, and with the help of ancient philosophers and modern neuroscientists, we can use our understanding of the brain—including its changing developmental stages—to not only survive, but also to thrive.

3. Music is both a metaphor for some of the most sublime workings of our human faculties and an actual agent of transformation. Music education and music as a paradigm for artful teaching are essential to schools.

The story that has guided my work with children and adults these past four decades is that we are luminous beings capable of extraordinary things, graced with elegant and expressive bodies, compassionate and feeling hearts, dazzling and imaginative minds and soaring spirits. These potentialities are given to us at birth in seed form, awaiting both our own efforts to realize them and our culture's efforts to encourage and support us in that task. Education is one of the ways a culture nurtures or shuts down, cultivates or lets go to seed, feeds or starves our possibilities. At its best, it "leads out and draws forth" (the original meaning of "educate") the full range of our promise. When teachers choose the things that help children train their body, open their heart, cultivate their mind, awaken their imagination and feed their spirit, we are on the right track. When we blindly follow the next trend to sweep through the schools, look at numbers instead of faces, leave the children out of our notions about what schools should be, we are lost.

This is the vision that has threaded throughout each day of my 44 years of teaching. But parallel with the commitment to a more inspired education has been a lifelong commitment to another path with heart—music.

THE THREAD OF MUSIC

My talent was modest, my ambition small and my musical path anything but straight and narrow, but still something kept music at my side ever since my first organ lesson at six-years old well over half-a-century ago. Some alluring melody kept calling me from ahead, some rhythmic pulse kept gently pushing me from behind and off I went time and time again in pursuit of some glimmering Siren call, luring me not to a crashing doom on jagged rocks, but to an exquisite room in the center of music's power and promise. In church basements, open verandahs, redwood decks, cozy kitchens, school gymnasiums, patient teachers helped me unveil the many voices of the Spirit in the form of Philippine Kulintang, Balinese gamelan, Ghanaian drums, Bulgarian bagpipe, Irish tin whistle, accordion, banjo and more. And always Orff xylophones in my music room and jazz piano in my living room. In my strange zig-zag journey, I always circled around the normal venues of musical training, missing out on the rigorous training of music degrees, the freewheeling experimentation of garage bands or the dues paid by endless nights playing piano in cocktail lounges. It took me decades before I dared claim the title "musician." And throughout it all, I kept wondering: "What does it all mean? Why do I bother? Why do I still work on improving, deepening and widening my musical expression?"

Perhaps it was the very eclectic nature of my development that gave me the habit of constantly questioning its purpose. It led me to not only wonder what music meant to my life, but to all lives. The combination of teaching, studying, playing and performing music got me thinking about music's role in human development, what it offers and what it doesn't, what is needed for it to fulfill the whole of its promise to all fortunate enough to be touched by it.

And so this book brings together a lifetime of teaching children and a lifetime of playing music with this startling premise: *that music is one of the most profound and effective ways to educate the whole child.* That it can only do so when the *teaching of music is wholly musical.*

And that when we understand what musical teaching feels, looks and sounds like, we can then *apply key principles to all of teaching*.

This notion is particularly challenging to those who have suffered through dull music programs—hard to imagine that working on one's squeaky clarinet tone or beating out quarter notes will create a new generation of Nelson Mandelas and Mother Theresas. For this to make sense, we need to take a moment to re-define what music is, what a musical music education looks and sounds like.

My life's work is based on the groundbreaking approach known as Orff-Schulwerk developed almost a century ago by composers Carl Orff and Gunild Keetman.* The essays in this book might be most easily understood and appreciated by my fellow Orff music teachers, giving new language and important details to this dynamic and child-friendly practice. Other music teachers may be intrigued to consider revising some of the default teaching methods of reading scores and mastering one instrument to win the competition. Classroom teachers may need to pause to try to translate musical examples to their situations, but any that know children well and recognize their own inspired moments of teaching can find much useful scaffolding for their intuitions and simple, clear and effective ideas as to how to plan their lessons to engage their students more fully. Finally, I would like to think that every reader, regardless of whether they are a teacher or musician, would find intriguing ideas, interesting information and new insight into the state of human culture and its possibilities for higher achievement and deeper healing.

The challenge of this premise is not only that we need to redefine what music is and what the musical teaching of music looks and feels and sounds like, but also that we need to redefine our notions of school and education. Paolo Freire once said:

> "Education either functions as an instrument which is used to facilitate integration of the younger generation into the logic of the present system and bring about conformity or it becomes the practice of freedom, the means by which men and

---

* See my book *Play, Sing & Dance: An Introduction to Orff Schulwerk*

women deal critically and creatively with reality and discover
how to participate in the transformation of their world." *

School as the place to practice freedom, to think critically and
imagine creatively, to participate in needed transformation of the
old, divisive, narrow, limiting, unjust ways—

that well describes my long years of teaching at The San Francisco School. Today, the pressure to conform seems greater than
ever and the bureaucrats are jumping over the school fence waving
their forms in their hands, but inside the sacred space of the music
room, the children still astound me with their remarkable selves,
daily demonstrate the power of music in their lives and constantly
inspire me to dig deeper and reach higher.

It is to them this book is dedicated.

---

* Freire, Paulo: *Pedagogy of the Oppressed:* Bloomsbury Publishing Inc: 2000

OVERTURE

It's Friday night. You come home from a hard week at work, put together a quick dinner, rush out in heavy traffic, circle about searching for parking and finally arrive at the concert hall. You squeeze past people to your seat, sit down to check your last messages before turning off the phone. The lights begin to dim and the buzzing crowd gets quiet. The concert is about to begin.

A moment of silence and the first notes of music fill the air. The busyness and business in your mind gives way to a bath of soothing sound, drawing you out of clock time into music time. You attend to the emerging conversation between the instruments, follow them as they swoop and slide and circle under and over and inside each other, note the different voices joining the discussion, feel the energies rise and fall in density and intensity. As you follow, your pulse slows or quickens, your breathing changes, the electric-chemical pulses of your nervous system start to fire and their motion creates e-motion, bringing your feeling life up to the surface.

You are now fully immersed in a world of profound meaning, where every note connects logically and inexorably to the next, where everything makes sense, where the chaos of the world is momentarily held at bay. The constant assault of random sensation is replaced by organized sound and motion, harmonious relations skillfully manipulated, carefully orchestrated tensions and releases.

The strings outside are sympathetically plucking the strings of the heart inside and you are flooded with the pleasure of good feeling. As the piece swells to a thundering climax or fades to a pin-drop quiet, you are lowered into that warm bath of soothing silence, a momentary soundless sound before the applause erupts. The concert is over.

And what precisely is everyone applauding? Not just the virtuosity and artistry of the musicians, but also the way they brought you out of the day-to-day, out of the ticking clock into a perpetual present, the way the music helped wash away the dust of the world and left you feeling cleansed and refreshed. For the moment, you feel a trifle more alive and alert and relaxed, a bit more loving and compassionate, a touch more connected and inspired and ready to face the grime and noise of the busy world. For a few brief moments, all gods are in their heavens and all's right with the world.

At least, until the guy in the parking garage cuts in front of you and you start angrily honking your horn. What happened to that harmonious feeling? As powerful as music is, it sadly doesn't stick to the ribs and effortlessly transform human beings into consistently self-fulfilled and loving people.

And isn't that a shame? But at least for the time it was playing, we were drawn into that perfect world. For as long as the music lasted, we remembered what it's like when the mind is happily sorting out pattern, the heart's strings are being plucked, the toes are tapping away and the imagination is romping through the fields of memory and fantasy. That's something. And worth the price of the concert ticket.

What makes music as wonderful as it is? How does it work? What separates it from business as usual? Can we bring the pleasure of the concert into other parts of our lives? Might we treat school as an uplifting rehearsal and performance? Not only re-affirm a commitment to music education, but to a musical education in which all subjects sing their way to understanding with deep pleasure? Can we consider what makes music so musical and in so doing, not only change the way we teach music, but also affect the way we teach everything? To aim for each day in schools to move like a piece of music?

That's the radical premise of this book. In these pages, we'll look at how to make music education more musical and consider what strategies can spill over to all subjects. We'll dream together of an artful approach to education that makes the venture more exciting, dynamic, effective and *fun* for the children.

And more interesting and fun for the teachers as well. Art and artful living refresh and sustain us, keep the flame of our passion lit without burn-out. And so does artful teaching. Everybody's happier when music is present. Let the concert begin!

CHAPTER 1:
THE CLASS AS MUSIC

- **ENTICING BEGINNING**
- **CONNECTED MIDDLE**
- **SATISFYING END**

Imagine going to a concert that starts like this:

> *"We're going to play six pieces. The first one is in E♭ major and you might notice how it modulates to the relative minor and then returns home again. The tempo of the second movement is slow and we want you to feel soothed by the sound of the oboe entering on bar 54. As the piece progresses…"*

The audience is already heading for the exit. They came to the concert to get away from words and hear some music. They're being handed the menu when they want the meal.

In actual concerts, the musicians gather a moment of silence, give a gesture, nod or countdown and voila!—the music begins. No need to explain—just begin and let the music speak for itself.

Imagine with me here that music class might begin in a similar way. That the teacher has spent an hour or two the night before not only preparing the content of the class, but dreaming how to begin it in a way that entices the students as powerfully as the opening notes of Beethoven's Fifth Symphony, Chuck Berry's *Johnny B. Goode* or

Miles Davis' *So What*. The students are drawn into a world beyond mere words. Their curiosity is awakened, their attention is sharpened and they're motivated to keep going and find out where it all is leading. That's what a musical beginning to music class can do.

Imagine with me yet further that teachers in all classes consider how to begin classes with a little twist that helps things feel something more than business as usual. That there is an artful approach to revealing the wonders to come, an enticing beginning that pays mind to children who enter a class curious about what they'll discover and eager to do something interesting. By taking beginnings as seriously as music does, the class takes on a different tone and both teacher and students are refreshed.

And from that beginning, both music and other classes develop like music, dancing with and around and through the stated opening theme. As the clock ticks toward the closing bell of the class time, all moves toward a culminating cadence that gives a satisfying closure. In short, the class "aspires to the condition of music" [*] and the students leave refreshed as they would from a concert.

THE WHOLE CLASS AS A PIECE OF MUSIC

"Teach like it's music" means imagining the *very class as a piece of music* with an **enticing beginning, connected middle** and **satisfying ending**. Your job is not only to know your subject area and transmit that information to the children, but also to artfully arrange your class so that the vital information unfolds like an intricate fugue re-stating its subject in different places or a sonata developing a theme or an improvised jazz blues swooping in and out of the chord changes. By putting as much—or more—thought into how you will artfully lead children to the edge of discovery, the class indeed can touch the children like a well-crafted piece of music and leave them feeling excited, refreshed and hungry for more.

It's surprising that this idea hasn't been more discussed in music education. Music teachers are trained to know about the following:

---

[*] English author Walter Pater once wrote: "All art constantly aspires towards the condition of music."

- Choosing repertoire.
- Teaching technique.
- Demonstrating care for the instruments.
- Developing musical literacy.
- Setting rehearsal procedures.
- Modeling strategies for greater expression in ensemble playing.

All of the above and more are important strategies to make the music in their classes more musical. But often our path to the music is profoundly unmusical. We shout at kids to settle down, take out their instruments, set up their music stands and warm-up with scales. They open their musical score and play measure 20 to 24, then stop, then try it again, then stop, then go to bar 29 to 42 and work on the dynamics and then stop and do it again and then —oops! Class is over! They put their instrument in the case, fold up the music stand, put away the chair, gather up their music folder and we remind them to practice pp. 2–5 at home.

Orff Schulwerk music teachers take a markedly different path to releasing music in the children. We begin actively with a sound or gesture, a rhythm or a text, a song or a dance, and set off to work with it. Starting from simple elements, we explore in our bodies and voices multiple possibilities that grow and develop. When done artfully, there is a sense of magic in the air. But since it's extremely difficult to teach as we have not been taught, even the most well-meaning Orff teachers get pulled back into the teacher habit of talking too much, of explaining too much, of stopping and starting in supremely unmusical ways.

Treating the class like a piece of music is a first step toward making the teaching of music more musical. And why stop there? Shouldn't every class have a beginning hook that gets the students interested, engaged, attentive and ready to jump in? Shouldn't each class in any subject have a sense of rhythmic stride as the students work, a feeling of one idea or activity connecting logically and inexorably to the next? And before having to leave the math mind to go to Spanish class or the art mind to go to P.E., wouldn't it be good to wrap up the various strands of the class's explorations to some sense of conclusion that satisfies like the closing chords of a refreshing piece of music?

In short, the music class—or any class—can be composed the way music itself is—with an enticing beginning that invites the children in, a connected middle that grows and develops and a satisfying end that announces the (temporary) end of the activity. Let's look at each of the three stages one at a time. *

ENTICING BEGINNING

Why are beginnings so important? Think about how you prepare for a first date or a job interview. Knowing that first impressions count, you pay a bit more mind to what you wear and how you look and how you'll present yourself. You understand that the beginning of any venture sets the tone for all to follow and proceed accordingly.

And so in art. What happens in the first bar of music, the first line of a poem, the first page of a novel, opens the door and points the way forward, announces a theme that will unfold and be sung back to. The more enticing it is, the more we are curious to follow and keep going.

And so it can be in our classes. The more inviting, mysterious and magical the beginning of any class, the more eager the students will be to step through the door into the lesson.

As all teachers know, attention is everything. Without the students riveted on you as you set things in motion, you have nothing. It is in our interest and theirs to begin with something that captures their attention. There are formulaic beginnings that offer a comforting familiarity ("once upon a time…"), there are beginnings that intrigue us ("it was the best of times, it was the worst of times, it was the age of wisdom, it was the age of foolishness…"), that surprise us ("a bright cold day in April and the clock was striking thirteen…"). There are dull beginnings that put kids in classrooms to sleep ("Today's class objectives are blah-blah-blah") and routine

---

* Practical suggestions for each will be found in the Interlude chapters.

beginnings that are neither soporific nor stimulating ("Take out your books and turn to page 30").

As we consider what kind of beginning to create, we would do well to remember that all people crave two opposing things—the comfort of the familiar and the surprise of the unexpected. Familiar routines give us the sense that there is order in the world, that amidst all the scary news or ups and downs of our emotional life, there is something we can count on. The world may be going someplace in a handbasket, but by gosh!, I know exactly where to sit in the circle and know that at 9:00 pm, it's time to take out the math sheet.

At the same time, isn't it wonderful when there is a little surprise or a change in routine? A new child is sitting in the circle and we don't know who they are or why they're here, but maybe they could be our new friend! We get ready to take out the math sheet and the teacher announces that it's too hot to work and the whole class is going to the beach. Yeah!! It's these small unexpected things that give a particular color and life to the day. As teachers, we can pay mind to both familiarity and novelty, create beginnings with some set, familiar routine leavened by an intriguing surprise twist.

Familiar routines are a common practice in schools. The teacher meets the children at the door, greets each with eye contact, a handshake and warm "hello," begins the day in a circle with some rituals like naming the day on the calendar, reporting on the weather, select sharings from kids and overview of the day's schedule. In specialty subjects like music or P.E. or art, the teachers will need to create the routine that makes the most sense for their class. The questions to consider include:

- How will the kids enter the class?
- How to establish personal contact with each kid and/or the group as a whole?
- Where will they go?
- How to signal the beginning of class amidst the chatter?
- How to start with something that meets their need for movement, engagement with material, social engagement?

- How might that change according to different age groups?

And then the surprise that brings enticement. How to get kids to perk up and notice that something interesting is about to happen here. A few general ideas to consider (with elaborations in Interlude I):

- Teach silently, using face, body and gesture to communicate all musical information.
- Teach in a different language that no students speak.
- Make a sculpture of whatever—books, pencils, drums, blocks, things the students will eventually use in the lesson—and circle around it like a museum art piece.
- Show an intriguing photo or painting.
- Tell a story that starts at A and takes a surprise left turn to Z.
- Make up a story with the kids in the story.

Textbook teaching methods are predictable, but the imagination is boundless. Use it!

CONNECTED MIDDLES IN THE CLASSROOM

Far too often, the way a music class develops is profoundly anti-musical—a constant stopping and starting that is antithetical to the very gift of music. Practice this measure. Stop. Do it again. Skip to measure 35. Stop. Back to measure 4. It's like driving through town and shutting off the engine at every light and stop sign. Not only does it wear and tear the engine and waste gas (uses more to start up than to keep idling), but it also is maddening to the flow of the drive. And yet this is often the way we teach our music classes. Stopping the action to say "Now we're going to…"

Flow is the backbone of the musical experience. The way one note tumbles into the next, the way the music heads unimpeded toward climax with its unique set of tensions and releases, is the great drama that keeps us listening. Once a piece begins, we may or may not wholly like the sounds, may prefer one theme over another, may not wholly understand the grammar and syntax of the choices, but still can be carried by the flow of it all. The one intolerable thing is to be interrupted—by the ringing cell phone, the sudden failure of the sound system, the music blown off the music stands in the outdoor concert. Nothing is more disturbing to our nervous system, which relies upon a dependable journey from the first note to the last. And yet time and again in the musical classroom, we disturb the flow. Of course, there are many times when we need to stop and start. Most music rehearsals, as well as solitary practice, require focusing on a particular passage and practicing it until we achieve the desired effect. There are many moments in my classes where kids are working out their parts and the resulting aural landscape is as far from harmonious flow as you can imagine! But still we should attend to the ratio of *how much time is spent preparing the music and how much music we are actually playing.*

Again, creating imaginative transitions within and between activities will do wonders to keep the class flowing and feeling like a piece of music. Some principal strategies to consider (with elaborations in Interlude 2):

- Keep the engine running, one musical part continuing softly while preparing the next step.
- Teach a simple part and keep layering in new information without pausing.
- Create a game to get kids to their place.
- Use rondo form to keep the music flowing.

SATISFYING ENDS IN THE CLASSROOM

"Once upon a time…" is the opening door in the old fairy tales that invites us into the story, signals the brain that we're entering a new time zone that is timeless, prepares us for a connected plot that unfolds and moves towards resolution, climax, a satisfying end. "And they lived happily ever after…" is the closing door that gently puts us back into clock time with that exhale of satisfaction, the feeling of refreshment that gives us energy to face again the workaday world. Without that sense of closure, the whole venture is incomplete and leaves us unsatisfied.

The end of class, like a piece of music, needs some ritual attention, some means of looking back and reflecting on what was accomplished and looking forward to what next need be done. Just like a handshake at the beginning of class is important to establish relationship with each student, so is some closing re-connection important. It's also a good time to offer some praise to the group as a whole as to went went well, some reminders about what could have gone better and why and a shout-out to individuals who had a shining moment. Just as a routine to enter the class is needed, so is there a routine to exit the class—first putting things away, cleaning up, lining up, etc.

Some strategies:

- Play through a piece or dance a dance in its entirety at least once in the class without stopping in the middle to fix things.
- Whether playing music, singing a song or performing a dance, insist on "the perfect ending"—at least five seconds with bodies frozen, voices quiet, instruments only sounding as the fading ringing last note.
- Close with a circle, reflecting with the students about what happened, what it meant, how it felt and what the next steps might be.
- Lead a meditative mindful activity to calm the body and mind before going to the next class.
- Find a musical way to move to the next class (as relevant).

LIVE LIKE IT'S MUSIC

Imagine with me here that all of life could be arranged to follow this pattern. That our very lives could unfold like music. Start with an enticing beginning—a healthy natural childbirth in a warm room with low light with welcoming loving parents and friends. Proceed to a connected middle—a life that has sense of purpose and destiny in which each event and choice proceeds comprehensibly to the next to help us realize our reason for being. Move toward a satisfying end—a natural death in a warm room with low light surrounded by loving friends, children and grandchildren ushering us out of this world and into the next.

Would that it were so! And sometimes it is. Sometimes children are born at home surrounded by family and friends and no complications. There are moments in our long life span when we feel in the groove, flowing effortlessly from one delight to the next, all the moving parts of our life in harmonious conversation and dynamic relation. There are some who pass from this world lying in bed at home surrounded by loved ones at peace with themselves and the life they have lived.

But truth be told, a whole life lived as music is far from reality. No one is a glorious symphony, raga or jazz improvisation from the first note to the last. We may be blessed with good fortune, helped by seen and unseen hands to keep our music playing in our lives, but such moments of grace come in fits and starts, if they come at all. Despite our best efforts, there are broken strings, stiff fingers, failed passages, notes out of tune, rhythms that don't mesh, band-members who are not listening, discordant tone clusters that can't find the resolving chord. Music is not a script to be followed, but an ideal to which we can aspire. You see how many words that describe good music—feeling a good *rhythm* to our day, being *attuned* with someone, attending a *harmonious* gathering—speak eloquently of the moments when we are graced with good living.

I don't want to claim too much for music—that it will effortlessly heal you and make you more whole and loving and connected, help you be a kinder and more compassionate person. But neither do I want to claim too little. The reality of making music, alone and with others, of creating music, of even just listening to music, can bring much comfort, solace, joy and happiness in our lives. When the music is in the groove and everyone's in tune, we have a few moments when the possibilities of our shared humanity are realized. The things needed to make good music—getting into the rhythm, being in tune, enjoying a harmonious consonance—are precisely the things needed to live well. What we can safely say is that it is a good idea in our lives *to aspire to the condition of music.*

And if you agree, why, then you need some successful musical experiences to understand what that might feel like. And to have those musical experiences means having access to some level of music education, be it in the family, community or school. And to have an effective music education means that every minute of your musical schooling is musical.

And that's why it's so important to "Teach Like It's Music."

SUMMARY

> **ENTICING BEGINNING: Create a hook that engages and leads to the main theme.**
>
> **CONNECTED MIDDLE: Plan transitions for smooth flow and development.**
>
> **SATISFYING END: Create a feeling of cadence to announce the end of class.**

CHAPTER 2:
THE CYCLE OF LEARNING

- **ROMANCE**
- **PRECISION**
- **SYNTHESIS**

Remember making airplanes out of spoons at the dinner table? Having long conversations with your dolls? Spending hours running away from waves at the beach or digging holes in the sand? As we grew into adulthood, we faced the serious demands of work and schedules and responsibilities and put aside our childhood ways. Yet those foundational experiences stayed with us our whole lives. They formed who we became

In a gem of a book titled *"WHERE DID YOU GO?" "OUT." "WHAT DID YOU DO?" "NOTHING."* How it was when you were a kid—and how things have deteriorated since." author Robert Paul Smith evocatively describes what childhood was like in the 1920's:

> "That was the main thing about kids back then: we spent an awful lot of time doing nothing. There was an occupation called 'just running around.' It was no game. It had no rules. It didn't start and it didn't stop... Many, many hours of my childhood were spent in learning how to whistle. In learning how to snap my fingers. In hanging from the branch of a tree. In looking at an ants' nest. In digging holes. Making piles.

Tearing things down. Throwing rocks at things. Spitting.
Breaking sticks in half. Unplugging storm drains, and drop-
ping things down storm drains, and getting dropped things
out of storm drains (which we called sewers.) So help us, we
went and picked wild flowers…Catching tadpoles. Looking
for arrowheads. Getting our feet wet. Playing with mud. And
sand. And water. You understand, not doing anything…." *

In my own childhood in the 1950's, my friends and I did similar
things. We played tag and hide-and-seek and skipped stones and
made forts from abandoned Christmas trees. We explored vacant
lots, climbed trees, caught falling leaves, choose up teams for
baseball and found a way to handle our disputes without a single
grown-up nearby. When it rained, we had books, records, cards and
board games to keep us busy. We were masters of self-entertainment,
experts at "just running around." TV was just kicking in and beginning to seduce us into passive screen-viewing and Little League was
starting to replace our independence with adult-organized play. But
mostly, a childhood spent "doing nothing" was still alive and well.

I believe we would have been happy to be left alone to play
our whole childhood. But then there was something called school.
Our four years of free play led us into a kindergarten that was still
kid-friendly—lots of finger-paints, story-times, playground time. It
lived up to its name, allowing us to be both weeds and flowers in a
garden of children.

But then came first grade. Suddenly there were rules and schedules that stopped and started. Whistling and snapping fingers were
considered useless, hanging from a branch dangerous, getting wet
unhealthy and doing nothing an offense when there was so much to
do—adding things, then subtracting them again, seeing Dick and
Jane going, then coming back again. There were things that had to
be learned and adults who never could quite explain why they had
to be learned. But we kids somehow understood that, Peter Pan
notwithstanding, we couldn't spend our lives "just running around
doing nothing"—there were newspapers to read, bills to pay, jobs

---

* Smith, Robert Paul: *"Where Did You Go?" "Out." "What Did You Do? " "Nothing."*
Norton & Company, NY, 1957, pp 92–93

to be worked, all of which needed the kind of knowledge that came from books and math worksheets. School was a necessary evil, to be patiently endured until the weekend or, joy of all joys! summer vacation. Occasionally, the two worlds came together —a report on our favorite book or science project probing the question we had always yearned to know. But mostly, there was school and there was summer and never the twain did meet.

I endured it all—reluctantly—for the next 12 years, but always felt that yawning gap between my playful curiosity outside of school and the regimented right and wrong answers inside of school. I wondered if the freedom of play and the discipline of work were really opposed to each other. If there could be a way for both to have a place at the school desk. If there might there be moments to take away the desks altogether.

Whitehead's Threefold Cycle
It was in a little book by the esteemed mathematician and philosopher Alfred North Whitehead that the whole matter became clearer. A series of lectures in the late 1920's was gathered into a book titled *The Aims of Education*, presenting some lucid ideas about learning that still ring true today.

Whitehead begins by questioning the notion that mental growth is a steady, ascending line from our First Reader to the Graduate Exam. He observes that "life is essentially periodic...there are periods of mental growth, with their cyclic reoccurrences...Lack of attention to the rhythm and character of mental growth is a main source of wooden futility in education." * He defines three basic stages of mental growth, each with its unique character and special needs.

First Stage: Romance
In this stage, we are buzzing with curiosity, trying to make sense of the world: we want to know what things are, how they work and why they are. The job of education, according to Whitehead, is a

---

* Whitehead, Alfred North: *The Aims of Education*; Macmillan Co. 1929; p. 17

"setting in order of a ferment already stirring in the mind." * The Stage of Romance is our first encounter with the physical world—the way blocks can stack and tumble, drum skins can sound, crabs can scuttle sideways. It is characterized by **possibility, wonder, excitement**. Its primary mode is **play**, particularly the kind of play kids do with dolls and blocks, sticks and stones. It is the time to generate the questions, to conjecture the hypothesis, to begin to experiment, without any pressure to obtain "correct" results.

Second Stage: Precision
Whitehead: "In this stage, width of relationship is subordinated to exactness of formulation. It is the stage of grammar, the grammar of language and the grammar of science…This stage is dominated by the inescapable fact that there are right and wrong ways, and definite truths to be known." †

Now analysis, drill, information-gathering, critical thinking become essential and we enter the arena of work, specifically schoolwork. The sequential curriculum, differentiated subject matter, textbooks, tests, mental and physical techniques, scientific procedures all make their home in this phase of the learning process.

Third Stage: Synthesis
Whitehead also calls this "Generalization" and describes it as "a return to romanticism with the added advantage of classified ideas and relevant technique." ‡ It is the fruition of precise training, the completion of the two previous stages in which *play and work, love and duty, romance and precision* are reunited higher up in the spiral of growth.

Each stage offers particular gifts to the learner. Artful teaching attends to the order of the stages and the conversation between them. Because such teaching cannot be packaged and systematically boxed, labeled and sold, there has never been a time when

* Ibid; p. 18
† Whitehead, Alfred North: *The Aims of Education*; Macmillan Co. 1929; p. 18
‡ Ibid; p. 19

schools as a whole clearly understood how to leave sufficient space for Romance, artfully craft Precision and culminate in a dazzling Synthesis. But there have been some useful models that have worked. The Romance of Kindergarten, extended recess and free choice. The Precision of diagramming sentences, working with mathematical formulas, digging into the scientific method. The Synthesis of a science fair project, musical composition, writing a play about an historical event. There are glimpses of these stages at work, but without a comprehensive understanding of how to gather them together in a purposeful pedagogy.

And now there are new obstacles to face.

Romance and Precision Today

Much has changed radically in the last 50 years. In the "old days" of "runnin' around," children mostly entered school armed with the gifts of four years of Romance. Today's children, some as young as one-year-old, are more apt to engage with a screen than with building blocks. They may come to kindergarten never having climbed a tree or put on a play with the neighborhood kids or jumped rope. They may already be loyal to their consumer product and have posters of rock stars on their walls. Four-year-olds may be playing on an organized team with uniforms and adults yelling at them to "kick the ball!" Minus the gifts of running around, skipping stones, sitting around and getting bored and then noticing the ants parading by, they are short-changed and robbed of Romance. Without that foundation, veteran teachers are noticing the decline in readiness, and every year, education becomes more and more remedial work.

When kids do enter kindergarten, they find a modified first grade. They may be more likely to sit at a computer in a cubicle than at a round table with a bunch of other kids. They may attend a school where recess has been shortened to prepare for the state-mandated tests and the arts have all but disappeared. With both parents working, kids of all ages might not get home unil 5 or 6 pm. They might eat a quick dinner alone or in front of the TV. They may have excessive homework as early as first grade and when they do have free time, they may already be addicted to machines.

Weekends for kids of all ages might be filled with wonderful opportunities like piano lessons, capoeira classes, soccer games and the like. But no matter how wonderful each opportunity can be, they start to add up to a childhood entirely scheduled and run by adults. Gone is the freedom of roaming around, figuring stuff out on their own, hanging out until something interesting comes along. Gone is time to tinker with things or pluck a guitar or walk in the woods. Things that a mere generation ago helped create world-changing people like Steve Jobs, Bob Dylan and Mary Oliver are now like an endangered species.

The erosion of Romance in childhood is not the only danger to effective education. Precision itself has suffered greatly in the feel-good culture that cares more about kids being entertained and feeling high self-esteem than subjecting them to the rigor of discipline. Kids in America today seem to know less than the generation before when it comes to things like grammar, spelling, vocabulary, not to mention the warhorses of times-tables, state capitols, cursive handwriting and the most basic things about history. The current model of public discourse in the media and the political realm is somewhere around the level of fourth grade in terms of vocabulary, coherent expression and the ability to understand basic ideas. A current President who refuses to acknowledge scientific fact—or any facts that he doesn't like—makes it difficult to inspire school children to aspire to intellectual competence. With a decline in both Romance and Precision, Synthesis has nothing to synthesize and no clear way to do so.

Solving these problems in the families and the culture at large is beyond any one person's power. However, the best place to begin is the place where we could have the most control and the perfect captive audience—school. Young children come to us with an imaginative, intellectual and humanitarian promise awaiting to be nurtured by thoughtful and caring teachers. A comprehensive understanding of how these three stages can revitalize education is a good place to start giving them what they deserve.

Romance in the School

To repeat: all learning needs a period—anywhere from five minutes to several years—of "messing around," of freely exploring and playing with objects, sounds, images, motions, ideas, a time of no right and wrong answers. Within certain margins of safety, children need to try things out without judgment or fear of failure or having to measure up to someone else's fantasy of excellence.

Recess and "free-choice time" in the class are two places where schools allow for such unstructured play. But teachers can also artfully create opportunities *within* their lesson plan. Before diving into the rich alliteration in Gerard Manly Hopkins' poem *Inversnaid*, take some time to scat-speaking explosive p's and sharp c's and breathy w's. Then the student is prepared to notice and appreciate phrases "pools so pitch-black," "in coop and in comb," "wildness and wet." Before teaching the techniques of basketball dribbling, throw some balls out on the court and observe how the kids figure it out. Before delving into pattern permutations, set out the Cuisenaire rods and watch what happens.

The great mistake—and one we often make—is getting too soon to the technical matters before sufficient exploration. You might hire an expert conga drummers to work with your kids only to discover that the students felt overwhelmed by too much information too soon and frustrated by the emphasis on correct techniques that were beyond their grasp at the moment. Instead, let them find as many different sounds on their drum as they can. Then they choose three of the best sounds and play their first name, last name and birthday using each of the three sounds. After each plays, the group echoes both the rhythm and the technique. The idea is simple, but musically effective and the child is delighted to bring something personal—name and birthday—to the activity and discover that it can make an interesting musical pattern.

In this exercise, the children often stumble on some of the classic techniques, but now with more sense of ownership and excitement. They've taken a path of exploration and arrived at a place of more precision. Now they're curious and excited for yet more. This is the time to bring in the expert conga player, to both demonstrate how the instrument can sound and show them how to get there.

In short, timing is everything. Going too soon to precision is like asking about wallpaper choices on the first date. When the timing is right, precision is a thing of beauty.

Precision in the School

Every field has its own technical vocabulary, its own particular procedures, its own long path to mastery. The Stage of Precision is the time to learn them. It's the time to set in order the multiple ferments unleashed in the Stage of Romance, to give names to the intuitive discoveries and shape to the ways of working. Most of the bars are set ahead of time at their preferred height and it is the job of the student to learn how to leap over them, the job of the teacher to train them to do so.

If Romance gifts us joy and delight, Precision grants us power. Once we can name something, once we can learn efficient physical techniques, once we habitually use time-tested procedures, we can better control our learning and direct our efforts. Bach takes on new meaning when we understand scales and harmonic progressions, math astonishes us with the way the numbers obey once we learn the correct formula, scientific method reveals that there is ordered thinking in a seemingly chaotic universe and it is within our grasp. No analysis of the grammar and syntax and dactyls of poetry alone will ever write a poem for us—we will need some solid Romance for that. But it will help us craft and shape and mold into more articulate coherence our hope to express clearly our experience.

Romance has no steadily ascending progress, no timetable to master the "5 Steps of Inspired Play," no easily assessable play standards that can grade us with an A or a B. Precision, by contrast, is a long and winding road with many markers of progress along the way.

Each mastered procedure or technique is assessable and measurable. Whereas play favors the brain's right hemisphere mode of absorbing everything at once, precision's work follows the left hemisphere's mode of sequential learning. First this, then that. Each technique mastered, each idea understood, then leads to the next higher level of mastery and thought. New learning stands on the shoulders of the previous learning as one ascends.

It may appear that Precision *replaces* Romance, but not so. Romance at any time and at any age should be kept close to give the needed whimsy and delight that adds color to the precise task at hand. If you want to delve into the abstract world of musical notation, you might begin with four kids standing in a line with legs together—Kai, Bob, Sue and Pat—and then add Sasha, Jasmine, Sally and Miles standing with legs apart. All recite and clap the rhythm of their names.

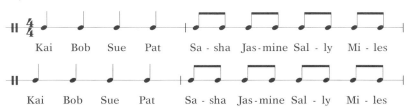

All eight kids then run around and reform the line in a new order. Voila! a new rhythm pattern for the class to clap!

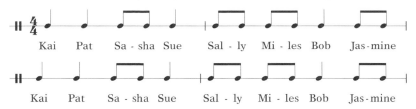

Transfer the living bodies to abstract symbols on the board (as above) and you've entered the precise work of notation with the playful romance of an imaginative exercise.

Here we arrive at the art of teaching—how to balance the Romance and Precision and note which the children need at any given moment. When we come to understand that Romance without Precision cannot fulfill its full promise, that Precision without Romance is dull and mechanical, our teaching changes dramatically. It is in the marriage of Romance and Precision where the finest work is born and that leads us to the third stage, Synthesis.

Synthesis in the Schools

Synthesis is the final exam of any unit of study. It is the place where play and work meet, where understanding is raised to new heights and rooted in new depths through the creative act. What began in the fertile fields of play and developed through the power of precise work now is ready to culminate in some kind of project chosen by the student. When students create something new—a music composition, a Science Fair experiment, a play about an historic event—that's when the information is most firmly embedded, most actively utilized and synthesized, most memorable. Students get to play creatively while demonstrating their grasp of "classified ideas and relevant techniques." Mastery of the taught techniques and information is evident in the work submitted alongside the student's passion, interest and ability to play with the material. That is the final exam that completes—temporarily—the full cycle of learning.

If **Play** is the key principle of **Romance**, and **Work** is the key principle of **Precision**, then **Create** is the key principle of **Synthesis**. Of course, children are remarkably creative in their fantasy play, but the creative energy of synthesis takes it to a new level of imagination. To cook the raw impulses of our playful creativity, we need the leavening of Precision. To have something worth cooking, we need the fruits of Romance. To finally serve the whole meal and share it with others is where Synthesis enters the process. All scientific discoveries, breakthrough inventions, artistic works are the results of a playful spirit dancing together with a rigorous disciplined knowledge to create something new and worthy in the world.

The Whole Cycle

"Genius is no more than childhood recaptured at will, childhood now endowed with the physical means to express itself,
and with the analytic mind to bring order into the sum of
experience…."*

—BAUDELAIRE

The French poet Baudelaire (who died in 1867, six years after Alfred North Whitehead was born) rightly intuited that the Romance
of childhood freely gifted should not be discarded, but transposed
to a new level as we grow into adulthood. Research indicates that
though the bulk of brain growth is in the first 21 years of our life—
the time of our schooling—new glial cells can still be formed in our
adult life and the pre-frontal lobes (seat of large ideas and compas-
sion) can continue to develop. Those who keep their vitality, sense of
wonder, alert minds intact as they age are those who have a lifelong
habit of creativity and investigation, who have kept playfulness side-
by-side with rigorous discipline.

And so whether you're 3 years old, 33 or 63, these tools of investigation are open to you. When entering any new learning at any
age, *play* first, mess around, explore, then *work* with the details of
concepts, procedures, techniques and finally *create* something new
from the synthesis of your play and work. *Play. Work. Create.* Note
the order in which they appear and keep them in constant conversation with each other.

Plan your classes with all three in mind. Look at your lesson
plan and see if you've left space for some measure of free play. Think
carefully about when to move to precision. Note when the children
are ready for some creative synthesis, both within the lesson in small
doses and near the end of a unit. Notice how this artful approach to
teaching makes sense to children, illuminates the subject and keeps
you dynamically engaged with your own passion to teach.

Play. Work. Create. Three simple words. Great results.

---

* Baudelaire, Charles: *Selected Writings on Art and Literature:* Viking 1972, p. 395

SUMMARY

ROMANCE/ PLAY
- Explore through play, no right or wrong answers
- Try things out following the body and intuition
- No existing bar to leap over

PRECISION/ WORK
- Work to gain greater control and mastery
- With the guidance of a teacher, learn classified concepts, systematic procedures and physical techniques
- Practice techniques, use procedures, apply ideas
- Learn and apply rules, with right and wrong answers
- Leap over a given bar

SYNTHESIS/ CREATE
- Return to exploration of Romance "armed with classified ideas and relevant techniques"
- Create something new, with no right or wrong, but fuller or less-full expression
- Set the bar to your desired height and leap over in your own style

---

ACTION:
Plan a lesson with an exploratory playful intro-duction, guide it toward precision and leave room for a short creative project or opportunity to improvise.

CHAPTER 3: 3D TEACHING

- **DO IT FIRST**
- **DISCUSS IT NEXT**
- **DO IT AGAIN**

When science first took hold of the Western imagination, some of its first prophets—Galileo, Newton and others—were searching for some unifying principle that would tie all the different disciplines together. They were looking for some magical philosopher's stone that would alchemically transform everything it touched to gold. They never did find it.

Don't we teachers all hope for the same? A magic formula that would turn the plain grey lesson plan into a shining and resplendent golden treasure? Alas, there is no magical philosopher's stone in education. But if we had to choose one principle that could unify all the separate threads of effective teaching and bring them together in a colorful cloth, it might be this: **Do it first. Discuss it next. Do it again.**

I move amongst what might be called progressive education circles, folks who value experiential education and hands-on learning. Yet still workshop after workshop, I find myself sitting in a little group asked to discuss the particular topic at hand—the psychology of the adopted child, diversity, gender equity, or what have you. In the egalitarian spirit of all voices being equal, we go around and

voice our opinion on the subject, take notes, share with the larger group, splash the ideas out on the butcher paper hung on the walls. *
I find myself restless and frustrated at the beginnings of these workshops and often unsatisfied at the end. And why? Because we're talking about something without having done anything, without a context, without a point of reference.

All of this could be solved by these three simple words—Do It First. Let's take them one at a time:

DO: Go to a playground and watch the children. They are incessantly "doing"—running, jumping, swinging, climbing, piling sand, poking bugs. Children are active creatures, perpetually exploring the world with their hands, bodies and senses. Then go to a café and watch adults. Chances are that they're not wrestling with each other, bouncing up and down on their chair, drumming with the silverware, making sculptures with their mashed potatoes. They are talking. Their physical involvement is often reduced to lifting the coffee cup to their lips, sending a text, signing the bill. No wonder kids think we're strange!

Kids *do*. Adults *talk*.

Of course, we adults also jog, do Pilates routine, work in the garden. We also have the hunger to do something and when we're engaged with the full measure of our body and senses, we feel better, we understand better, we live better.

And so the magic central principle of education, whether it be for kids or adults:

"Stop talking and do something!"

IT: What that "it" is, the particular something the children will do in your class, will need to be carefully thought out. Trained in the paradigm of education as mere explanation, we think that just saying or reading words is enough. It's not. We need to think about

---

* Whatever happens to that butcher paper anyway? Where does it go? Who ever looks at it again?

how to make a point come alive as a tangible and physical activity. *
"Gesture the shape of the melody, draw an idea, dance a concept" is
mostly how we were never taught, but is precisely what will activate
and animate the children.

FIRST: With children, it's always a good idea to begin from where
they are, and play is where they almost always are. It's their primary
mode of exploring, engaging with, making sense of the world. Any
class that has an element of play is ten steps ahead of the game. By
beginning with play, the children are more receptive to whatever
work you have in store for them. Start with an activity and you set
the foundation for discussion, warm up the body and mind for the
main theme, set the tone for fun and social interaction.

DO IT FIRST. But don't stop there. Once having played the game,
now is the time to sit down and talk about it. The discussion will be
much more meaningful having had that experience first.

DISCUSS IT NEXT

> "We do not learn from experience. We learn from reflection
> on experience." †
>
> —JOHN DEWEY

In my world of Orff Schulwerk, learning by doing is a central
pedagogical principle. At an Orff workshop, you put down your
pen, take off your shoes, get up and come into the circle. You play
instruments, sing and dance. That's what attracts people to the
Schulwerk, that sense that in a world where we spend so much time
talking *about* things, here we're actually doing the thing itself. We're
not learning about music by talking about it, we're learning about
music by making music and better yet, actively *creating* it. People

---

* For a brilliant example of this principle at work, look up $100 Race on YouTube. Here
is a concrete, physical activity that shows how privilege works in our culture and drives
the point home deeper than any mere discussion ever could.

† Here you have the challenge of reading about this in a book without having taken
the workshop. It's difficult to re-flect on something before you've flected! And why isn't
"flect" a real verb?

continue to come back to workshops because it feels so good to get up and move and make music with people. By experiencing themselves the seamless process the teacher embodies, they're now ready to duplicate it in their teaching with the children.

At least, that's what I used to think. In the Orff Schulwerk summer training courses I teach, I saw that after three summers of excellent modeling from our inspiring teachers, the Level III students teaching a sample lesson had not yet fully understood the essentials of teaching in the Orff style. They benefited from that process as students, but didn't yet understand how to transfer it to their own teaching. How could this be?

The answer was simple: Experience alone is not enough. They needed to **reflect** on the experience, **name** the principles and **codify** the details. When I began to share the details of how I plan and teach a class, it changed everything. Their lessons began to show the same kind of flow and imagination our teaching staff embodies, but in their own personal style and voice. *Now* they were prepared to share it with their students.

In our own classes with children, we also need to leave time for some reflection. "What did we do? How did we do it? Why did we do it? What might we do next?" Having answered some of these questions, named and made conscious the concepts experienced immediately and intuitively, the children are now ready to do it again and take it all to a higher level.

DO IT AGAIN: I often call this kind of work "toes-up learning." The music comes alive first in the tap of the toe and then propels the feet to move through space, gets the hips twitching, the hands clapping, voices singing, finally arriving at the head. Perhaps this is why nature placed our head at the *top* of the body, suggesting that it is the last to join the party. "Hey, what's going on down there?" the brain wants to know and quickly categorizes and connects and organizes and names all the information and then sends all the signals back down again. Now, with a more conscious understanding, the body can return to its party of physical, sensual and emotional delight and do it all yet better and enjoy it all one inch deeper.

In the music class, this means beginning with a musical experience. Just play. Sing. Dance. Then reflect on what happened. Give names to the key concepts and techniques. Then return to making music with a new and more conscious understanding.

Do it first. Discuss it next. Do it again. The 3D's take education out of the flat world of mere explanation into the full three-dimensional world of experience married with reflection.

The Importance of Context

How might these ideas apply to other subjects? The poet David Whyte tells a story about one of his University professors who entered class one day, shook a student by his jacket collar and said, "There are people in this world who will hate you just because of the cut of your face. And there's nothing you can do about it!" Then the teacher strode to his desk while the class tried to recover from the shock, turned to them and said, "Now we're ready to talk about Iago and Othello."

In today's educational climate, that teacher might be fired for physical abuse or marked down for not clearly stating the class's objectives. In my book, he gets the Nobel Prize for teaching. Besides shaking the students out of their customary slumber, he took a commonplace school subject and made it deeply real and personal. He created a context that shook the students to the marrow and made them wonder: "Might somebody hate me even though I didn't do anything to them? Why would they? How am I going to deal with that? Guess I'll dive into this archaic language and see if Othello has any good advice."

Without context, school becomes a dull exercise going through the moves of someone else's agenda. Before schools, children raised on the farm or in the forest or fishing village got a natural education that always had a context. "Here's how you catch fish, here's how you milk the cow, here's how you snare a rabbit. Here is the plant that

Doug Goodkin

heals you, here is the one that kills you." In short, *survival* was (and still is for many) the context and a pretty high motivating factor—no clever devices are necessary to engage the attention of the student.

But in the complex cosmopolitan cultures, where people of markedly different traditions and values are thrown together, we have often lost the context of our educational endeavors. No child in a hunting society ever asks, "Why do I have to learn how to hunt?" but day in and day out, children perpetually wonder why they have to learn about the square root of 36 or the Spanish-American war. The idea that learning to read, multiply and memorize the dates of the big battles is necessary for survival is too abstract for a young child (and even older ones). Especially today when machines do our math and correct our spelling, a constant diet of images on screens makes reading feel tedious and history means yesterday's soundbite, it may be difficult to convince young people that school is a worthy endeavor.

Hence, the need for introducing *context* in a lesson is more important than ever. A teacher who can bring the timeless concerns of people into even the most mundane lesson is a teacher who will have the kids sitting up in rapt attention. Kids may not think they're interested in a Tai Chi lesson, but they are always interested in finding out what their body can do. They might think math is boring, but they are always intrigued by what patterns their minds can perceive. They might think a song is corny at first, but they are certainly interested in what feelings their hearts might hold. If we begin with the premise that children come to us alive and alert, brimming with curiosity as to how the world works and what their part in it is, then we can give every lesson a context that satisfies their curiosity.

This may be as close as we'll get to the philosopher's stone of education. In alchemy, the stone was believed to be an elixir of life, a carrier of rejuvenation, transmuting everyday metals into rare and valuable gold. Once you begin to craft lessons that start with engaging and playful activities, lead to meaningful and useful discussions and return to an activity rejuvenated by the whole process, you will note see a remarkable change in the children.

What better gift to bequeath to them?

SUMMARY

DO IT FIRST: Create an activity that generates introduces a topic, generates questions, provides a context for further investigation.

DISCUSS IT NEXT: Reflect on the experience of that activity, name the questions, investigate the answers.

DO IT AGAIN: Return to activity with new knowledge and a summary of key learning in media of choice.

ACTION: Plan a lesson with a concrete activity—a game, a drawing, a movement exploration, a drama improvisation—without specifically naming the topic to be studied. Ask the students to imagine the theme and discuss the things that came up. Return to the opening activity with the new information.

INTERLUDE I:
ENTICING BEGINNINGS

Clear thought and coherent vision make a tangible difference in our teaching. One good idea thoroughly understood can fuel scores of inspired classes. Yet we also need concrete models and practical examples. Here is the first of three interludes in this book that highlight the details of the ideas set forth in Chapter 1—the enticing beginnings, connected middles and satisfying ends. They are offered as models to adapt as needed to your own particular teaching situation and in your own style. You'll note that I tend toward the playful, game-like way of teaching important life skills. I've found that offering a challenge like "Who can…?" often works more effectively with children than "Do this!" These models may also serve to help you look more closely at your own routines and procedures you've established and consider which might be refined or enhanced.

SELECT OPENING ROUTINES IN THE EARLY YEARS
The Neat Shoe Club

"A place for everything. Everything in its place."
—MARIA MONTESSORI

Learning how to take care of things is a lifelong skill best introduced young. How to neatly hang up one's coat, put things in one's cubby or locker and so on. Creating a routine for children to practice these things is an important part of schooling. Making a playful game of it is one way to make it fun and effective at the same time.

Because children take off their shoes in my music class, they need some kind of opening routine. Enter "The Neat Shoe" club. Membership is earned by putting the two shoes neatly side-by-side. While the last kids are getting their shoes off, I'm the Inspector General seeing who renewed their membership. When the last shoes are lined up, we're ready to go—often with an opening dance or follow-the-leader parade. They get up and start moving and their shoes are left behind, in a neat and orderly row sure to impress any visitors who enter the room.

Classroom teachers might form a Neat Cubby Club or Organized Binder Club, complete with membership cards, a president and a end-of-the-year certificate.

The Parade

> "I lay it down as an educational axiom that in teaching you will come to grief as soon as you forget that your pupils have bodies."
>
> —ALFRED NORTH WHITEHEAD

Preschool kids are a constant reminder of Whitehead's observation, so it is best to get them moving from the start. After the shoes have been lined up, grab a drum and invite the kids to the parade, following you around the room moving to the beat. When the drum stops, all "Freeze!" Don't forget to point out the most interesting shapes—the more extravagant the shape, the better! That will inspire the others to impress you with their imaginative solutions.

This is also a good time to vary the locomotor movements with appropriate drum accompaniment—marching, galloping, jumping, tiptoeing, skipping, slow motion walk and so on. Lead the parade line to eventually form a circle and on the last "Freeze!" melt down slowly and there you are, ready for the next phase of class with kids seated in a circle. They've arrived there energetically, effortlessly, attentively and are now ready for the next part of class, typically a rhythmic chant or song or game.

In addition to the hand-drum parade, the beginning of class is an excellent time to build a repertoire of songs with motions and folk dances. A song like the *The Wheels on the Bus* or *Little Red Caboose** gets the kids moving, singing and motioning all at once. Simple folk dances like Cherkassiya offer a body percussion A section and moving with different motions B section. As the children grow comfortable with this material, select kids can lead the parade and choose the motions as needed.

Finally, there are other games like *Old King Glory* or *There Is Somebody Waiting for Me* that get the kids out to the floor one at a time. Some games like *Everyone Born in January Skip Around* will get small groups out on to the floor one birthday month at a time and then stay out to freely dance to the other verses.

Sitting Postures

Keeping in mind the cardinal truth of young children's restless bodies, we will need to pay attention to how the kids are sitting in the circle. Again, with a playful atmosphere in the forefront, a quick series of challenges will keep the kids engaged and moving: "Who can sit long sitting? Hook sitting? One leg hook sitting, one long sitting? Switch! Switch in slow motion. Don't switch. Kneel sitting. Side kneel sitting. Butterfly sitting. Long arms, butterfly legs. Switch. Criss-cross applesauce!" †

---

* Rather than include these songs, dances and games here, go to your nearest YouTube channel!

† I'm indebted to P.E. teacher Rudy Benton for many of these sitting postures and their importance.

Off we go with the chant, *"Criss-cross applesauce (3x) Pepperoni Pizza!"* * and then move on to the next activity. The kids are seated in that solid cross-legged postures, we're ready for the next part of the class.

Assigned Places

The free-flowing nature of music class is a challenge for some children. Kids, like adults, like to claim a little piece of territory that they feel is theirs and places them concretely in the space—a place at a table, a desk, a seat in the car and so on. Some kids do fine with being anywhere at anytime, others find it difficult. To help offset that freewheeling freedom, I give kids a special spot on the rug, spaced equally apart in rows and columns and all facing the front. Assigned places in the music room achieves three worthy things:

1. It gives children the comfort of their own personal space.
2. I choose where they sit, putting kids up front who need to be close to me, separating kids who distract each other, balancing the male and female energies.

---

* A complete lesson based on this rhyme is in my book *Intery Mintery*.

3. The frontal arrangement is excellent for left-right mirroring, the rows and columns an easy way to do things in parts or canon.

To establish places, we play a simple away and back game. To sung, played or recorded music, the kids move away from their place, but they must return by the final note of the song. These are important skills, connecting time (when do I get back?), space (how far should I go before I need to start heading home?) and energy (can I walk far away and then run home on the last phrase?). The challenge of getting home on time is fun, the active dance is just right for their energetic bodies and their style of moving to the particular music is part of their overall training.

3D	3C	3B	3A
2D	2C	2B	2A
1D	1C	1B	1A

OPENING ROUTINES IN THE OLDER YEARS

With the older students, I used to think they were mature enough to just enter the class, grab a stool and gather in a circle. Not so. They'd wander around the room, look for bigger stools or different chairs, wander to the instruments and start playing. In short, it was not an enticing beginning. Finally realizing **they needed the same structure and routine as the preschoolers**, I created some and stuck with them. It changed everything.

The Handshake

All kids want to feel seen, known and valued and taking time at the beginning of each class to greet them with a personal handshake is a clear and simple way to show them they're important.

Make sure you remind them that eye-contact is part of the routine. I teach the kids a special handshake from Ghana that takes a bit of practice, so it's both a good way to make contact with each student personally and also give them a physical skill to work on. *
After the handshake, they sit in a pre-determined place.

The Group Greeting

Children often come into a room chatting and talking and that is natural. A routine and ritual greeting signal is needed to mark the true beginning of class.

With the 8th grade, I've developed a tongue-in-cheek routine that they enjoy. I have taught many of these children for 10 years and following our school practice, they have always called me "Doug" (or "Dougie" in the preschool years). But now I tell them they will have the honor of formally addressing me as Mr. Goodkin. Once all are settled, I face them and say with an energetic voice, "Good morning, class!" They rise in unison, put their hands together as if they were singing in a formal choir and answer in one voice, "Good morning, Mr. Goodkin!" It is a playful routine that they seem to enjoy—for the entire year! When they sit down, class has officially begun. This simple routine has worked wonders. *

The Preparation

How does one teach parts by rote without a score? I often begin like this:

- With the xylophone turned to face the students, I demonstrating a simple part. (This means I have to learn the part backwards—my right is their left. A good skill to develop!)
- They watch and sing the pattern while I play.
- As above, miming the mallet technique in the air.
- One at a time, they come up and briefly try out the part before going over to the instruments, choosing one and beginning to practice. (If they're not ready, I'll correct them or have them wait). You might also put out two or three instruments like this to make the process go a bit faster.

---

* I once saw a video of a teacher who greeted his students with personalized complex handshakes, each one different than the rest. Impressive!

- Once at the instruments, I encourage them to pair up with someone who might learn the part a bit faster and will help them out.
- After a few minutes of aural chaos with everyone practicing at their own time and pace, I need a signal for quiet so we can all play in unison. And that leads us to:

"Mallets up!!"

The first one up is the "Winner" and the last one is on "probation." If they're last the next time, I take their mallets away and they play with their fingers. If they're the winner twice in a row, they get extra (imaginary) points. * This playful approach helps to re-focus the group after the period of necessary musical chaos as they work on their parts.

---

* I tell them the story of the remarkable 8th grader Harriet who was first *every class the whole year!* And challenge them to match her record.

INTRIGUING BEGINNINGS FOR ALL AGES
Teaching in Silence

Imagine a class that begins without the teacher talking, yet leading the group through a variety of activities that end in a complete musical experience 20 minutes later without a word being spoken. Wouldn't it capture your attention? Not knowing what was coming next, might you have been more wholly engaged and alert? Would you be astounded at how much music was made without a single verbal direction given?

How was information conveyed? The way the conductor of the orchestra does it—through gesture, facial expressions, eye contact, rhythmic energy in the body. The way the musician does it—singing a phrase for the group to follow or playing a rhythm, with the energy, inflection, gesture, body posture joined to the notes. The things that give life to music—attack, touch, tone, phrasing, dynamics, rhythmic flow—are communicated directly instead of symbolically with >, <, ^, *pp* or *f* s. More immediate, more effective, more musical. Teaching in silence is more than a neat parlor trick—it's a way for the teacher to learn how to embody the music and transmit essential knowledge through conducting and modeling rather than explaining.

Teachers in general simply talk too much and music teachers in particular need to watch their words. When something can be communicated faster, more effectively and more directly through sound and gesture, stop talking and just *do* it. If you find yourself saying "Now we're going to…" you have spoken four words too many. Don't tell us what we're going to do. Just do it!

And so a reminder to all my fellow music teachers. Use your words sparingly and get right to the music. You will be teaching music musically and your kids will start to understand that the way they're learning music and the music itself are aligned with each other. What they do and the way that they do it are of one piece. Once you learn to habitually teach this way, it will change everything.

Teach in a Different Language

There's a little clapping game I learned from two little girls in Chile and whenever I teach it in a workshop, I tell the story of how I learned it. In Spanish. In the telling, I speak slowly, emphasize key points with gestures, I repeat and re-phrase sentences, I accent familiar-sounding words—*universidad, Mamá, foto*—and generally just act out the little story. I then ask someone in the group who doesn't speak Spanish to re-tell the story in English. It's remarkable how well they do! And they're surprised by it as well.

By using the same strategies as in silent teaching—talking with hands and face and now vocal inflection—we can communicate a great deal. And in so doing, change the quality of listening. As soon as the students hear a different language, there is a moment of surprise and the attention ratchets up a notch. Voila! We've created an enticing beginning.

This approach is yet another signal that something different is happening here, with two added side-benefits:

1. They can actually begin to learn some words and phrases in the spoken language.
2. They can develop empathy for new children in the school who are not native English speakers.

    If you speak another language, try it. If you don't, make one up.

hello   habari gani

bonjour   hola

konnichiwa

buon giorno   SALAAM

55–38–7

Albert Mehrabian, a UCLA psychology professor, came up with the 55–38–7 theory of communication. * He claimed that in many communication situations, 55% of the message you receive comes from the body language of the speaker—their posture, gesture, facial expression. Imagine someone telling you they love you with an angry face and an aggressive stance. What would you believe, the words or the body?

38% comes from the tone of voice—timbre, inflection, accent. Tone can literally change meaning. "Great!" with a sarcastic sigh means something different from "Great!" with an enthusiastic smile. The rising intonation of "You want to go now?" means something different from "You want to go now." The accents "You want to go now." "You want to go now." "You want to go now," all create different meanings.

---

* One must question his methods to arrive at such precise numbers and I'm sure that there is no way to scientifically quantify these things. But it's fun to treat it as if it were literally true and use it to convey the general truth to those who like things neatly summarized mathematically.

A mere 7% of meaning comes from the actual words being said. But still words are important! I remember once being carried away by the energy and excitement of a preacher at a Gospel church and then realized that I didn't agree with anything he was saying.

Naturally, the 55-38-7 rule doesn't apply to all situations. Giving instructions on how to set up your cell phone, for example, doesn't require much beyond the words themselves. But in any interaction involving emotion, the kind of talk you hear in public speaking, sales, political campaigning, preaching in a church—and teaching in a class—will lean heavily on the musical elements of speech. How you dance your meaning, support the words with your hands and face, how you sing your meaning and support your meaning with the rise and fall of your voice, the tempo, the phrasing, all factor into how effectively you communicate to the students. "Teach like it's music" also means speak like it's music. If you're not sure what I mean, listen to a 3-year old tell a story.

Imagine Martin Luther King's "I Have a Dream" speech spoken with a flat, newscaster affect without the rhythmic phrasing and rise and fall of his tone. The words might be the same, but they wouldn't reach us or affect us the same way. It is important what you say, but often it is equally—and perhaps more—important how you say it. We would do well to train our teachers to note their posture, work on their diction and phrasing and attend to the music of their communication style. I predict their class might be 55% + 38% more engaging.

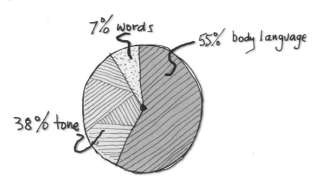

Make It Physical

Schools everywhere cover the walls with words like these: Excellence. Effort. Kindness. Teamwork. Respect. Long lists of lovely nouns reminding the young people how we'd like them to be (mostly because we were not!). In all my travels, I've never seen words like "Violence. Injustice. Meanness. Laziness." It seems that schools everywhere pay lip service to the same values. That's a good starting point.

But a noun is a noun, it just sits there inertly and can't penetrate to the heart of the child. It's a starting point, but powerless until transformed to the verb of the daily round of how teachers treat kids in schools, how kids treat each other, how systems are set up in place to actually draw forth those lovely potentials. The development of moral character and good citizenship is a lifetime's work built from the accumulation of a daily practice. But a good place to start is to make the desired values concrete and physical.

Simply holding hands in a circle is already a form of teaching. The group is physically connected and linked, each person feeling the warmth of their neighbor's hands. All are equally visible, no one can hide, yet no one is elevated or stands out from the rest.

Want to introduce the idea of Respect? Lead the circle to the middle and bow. Affectionate intimacy? All turn and give their neighbor a little back massage. Switch directions. Trust? All link arms and lean back, holding each other's weight.

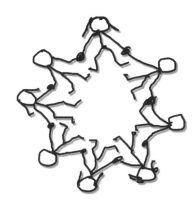

Connection. Respect. Attention. Physicality. Affection. Trust. Now all these worthy nouns have a physical counterpart, a concrete experience in the body to refer back to. When trust is broken in one way—like a child laughing another child's effort—there's a way to talk about it. "Remember when we leaned back in a circle holding each other? What you just did was take your arm away and made this child fall down. It not only hurt him, but it hurt all of us, because now the circle of trust is broken. And it hurts you, because you will need us to hold you in this class." As you are making your class agreements, it would serve you and the children to think about how to make each one concrete and physical.

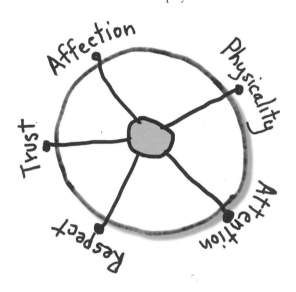

Tour the Art Gallery

The students enter the room and something is different. On the circle time rug are percussion instruments assembled like a sculpture. Curiosity is now awakened. What is that? Why is it there? And what are we going to do with it? You begin the class with some familiar routine—roll call or some such thing and pay no attention to the thing in the center so that their little minds can keep percolating. At just the right moment, you ask, "Anyone notice anything different today? Why do you think it's there? What do you think we're going to do with it?" Enticing beginning.

Off we go with some sort of counting-out game to choose people to take an instrument one at a time from the sculpture and begin playing something. As the visual sculpture grows smaller, the aural soundscape grows larger. Enticing beginning!

Consider what kind of sculpture might work for your class, what object to put down in the middle of the circle or on the table at the front of the room. Like a globe with a chocolate bar on top and the students guessing what it means. "Maybe today we're going to see where chocolate is grown and how it gets to us. And whoever learns the most gets to eat the chocolate bar!" Mystery, Enticement. Surprise. Motivation for wonderful things to happen without explicitly promising a reward for good behavior.

Start with *This* to Get to *That*

To talk about one thing, begin with something else. Not always. But remembering that you have 30 seconds to capture the kids' attention before they reach for the remote, it's a good strategy to keep in your back pocket. This more circuitous route to the main point invites the imagination to partake, like a joke heading for the punch line or a piece of music dancing around a melody before openly stating it.

When the 8th graders walk into my Jazz History Class and sit down for yet another class in a day that bounces them back and forth between humanities, math, science, P.E., art, Spanish and more, they're not breathless with anticipation awaiting my opening words. In fact, they often have no idea what I will present to them today and besides juggling all those other subjects in their head, they're also 8th graders deeply entrenched in their social peer group, dealing with the inevitable hierarchies of who's in and who's out, worried about their high school visit the next day, finding themselves attracted in a different way to some of their peers. How to engage them in my lesson? Here's one sample:

> "Imagine you are a social worker and a case study comes across your desk. Here is a young boy living in a poor neighborhood so violent it's called The Battleground. His father left him, his mother scrapes by doing menial labor, he himself has to go out working by the time he's 6 selling coal in the Red Light district. When he's 12, he shoots a gun in the air during a New Year's celebration and gets taken off to reform school for two years. He never returns to school, gets married at 18 years old to a prostitute. To top it off, he's a black man in a brutally racist society. What kind of future do you predict for this young man?"

From that beginning, you introduce them to one of the most famous figures of the 20th century—Mr. Louis Armstrong. The kids at my school are very open-minded and curious, but I know they didn't wake up that morning wondering about Louis Armstrong. I needed a hook to engage their attention. The above worked well—I started off talking about *this* and ended up talking about *that*. And the kids were with me.

Mystery and surprise make learning more enjoyable, interesting and memorable. Consider it.

Personal Story

In another 8th grade Jazz History Class, I held up a blank square of cardboard and announced to the kids, "This changed my life" and had them guess what it was and why it was so important to me. I then turned it around and showed the record cover of Scott Joplin's music. I told them the story of first hearing this record while in college and how it led me through the door into the house of jazz. And off we went to talk about Scott Joplin and the movie *The Sting* and the piece *The Entertainer* and the sheet music industry and the role of pianos in pre-radio culture and what Jelly Roll Morton did with *The Maple Leaf Rag* and the thousand other themes that a single life story can touch. All from a single square of cardboard. And a little story that told the kids what it all meant to me. By sharing my passion, it just might touch their own.

Education as mere data and information can be dull, dry and boring, but when teachers share a story about what something means to them, it becomes infectious and brings the subject alive in a new way. That's not a bad definition of our job as teachers—to joyfully infect our students with our own passion and enthusiasm.

So why not enter the subject du jour with a little personal story? It helps cultivate intimacy, vulnerability and personal relationship when you share appropriate and relevant stories from your own life. Tell the kids how you came to love what you love and see how that raises their own excitement about the subject.

Invented Story

It has been raining for five days and the kids in school are going crazy. Your most challenging class is about to enter and you are wondering if you've used all your sick days and surely that cough you have is getting worse. Now's the time to reach into your back pocket for the perfect enticing beginning.

> "Kids! Come gather around, I have an amazing story to tell you! Are you ready?

> Well, you know I've worked at this school for a long time and I've seen a lot of incredible kids and wonderful classes. But I never met a class like the one I taught ten years ago. These kids were so amazing that one time it rained for ten days straight!! Ten days!! And you know how we all get restless when we can't play outside? Well, these kids came into my music class and I

thought they'd be running around and going crazy. But they didn't! They came in so quietly that I didn't even notice them. I was looking in my book and when I looked up, there they were, sitting perfectly still and quiet and looking at me waiting for me to give them a direction. And then when I started singing a song, they all joined in and sang it so quietly and beautifully. Let's see if you could sing like they did. "Twinkle twinkle little star…" Wow! That was pretty good!

Well, then I played the piano and they did some movement and they always did a "Freeze!" in a perfect shape at the end of each piece. And they never once used their voice or bumped into each other. I've been looking for a class as good as them for ten whole years! And I've never found one. But maybe you will be that class! And then I'll tell a story about you ten years from now! What do you think? Can we do it? Good luck!"

Maybe they will and maybe they won't, but I guarantee the class will be 100% better than if I told the kids, "I know you're antsy from the rain, but you better be good in my class today or else!!!"

Once you commit yourself to the idea that creating enticing beginnings is worthy of your time and effort, the right choices for the right activities at the right time will begin to appear. And both you and the children will be happier for having made the effort.

SUMMARY

NEAT SHOE CLUB: Create a routine for caring for things.

- PARADE: Begin actively, develop folk dance repertoire, get kids effortlessly into a circle.
- CRISS-CROSS APPLESAUCE: Give names to sitting postures.
- ASSIGNED PLACES: Give a personal space in the music class.
- HANDSHAKE: Make personal contact with each student.
- GROUP GREETING: Create a ritual beginning greeting.
- MALLETS UP! Invent a playful routine to get attention during instrumental ensemble.
- TEACHING IN SILENCE: Get the children's attention and communicate musically without words.
- DIFFERENT LANGUAGE: Try another way to get attention.
- 55-38-7: Teach with body, gesture, facial expressions and musical speaking voice.
- MAKE IT PHYSICAL: Communicate abstract ideas with hands-on concrete activities.
- THE ART GALLERY: Prepare the space and see things from a new perspective.
- FROM THIS TO THAT: Create mystery and surprise by starting one place and unexpectedly arriving at another.
- PERSONAL STORY: Cultivate relationship with the group by sharing relevant personal stories.
- INVENTED STORY: Create class expectations through the vehicle of story.

ACTION:

Make a list of your own routines and strategies to engage children more fully. Consider trying one of the above and note the result.

CHAPTER 4—THE 4H CLUB: HAND, HEART, HEAD, HEARING

Historically, school's primary task has been to cultivate the mind. From Plato onwards, people who merely worked with their hands were considered in a lower intellectual class, as were people whose lives were led by their heart (note Plato's disdain of poets). But modern brain research affirms what enlightened thinkers have long known—the hand and heart are inextricably connected to the head, and all three mutually affect each other in profound ways. The trio of hand, heart and head brings us to a fuller dimension of education. *

The three are wholly present in every subject area with different degrees of weight—math with a bit more head, poetry with a bit more heart, basketball with a bit more hands. Music needs all three in just about equal proportions—and with one extra H: Hearing.

---

* Science is now looking at these faculties from the neuroscientific viewpoint of how the brain develops and functions. Frank Wilson's *The Hand*, Antonio Damasio's *Descartes' Error*, and a gem of a book by three doctors—Thomas Lewis, Fari Amini, Richard Lannon—titled *A General Theory of Love* all illuminate the separate, but connected functions of hand, head and heart. These insights could have a profound effect on education if we put into practice the insights as to how the senses, body and emotion help cultivate the mind. Or if we recognized the various enlightened pedagogies that already understand these ideas—Montessori, Waldorff, Orff Schulwerk and more. Where the current insights affirm such proven practices and give us new language, we can happily continue along those paths with increased understanding. Where they suggest new turns or lead us to reconsider what we're doing, they likewise will help contribute to the well-being and intelligence of the children we teach.

To be a successful musician means you'll need to pay your dues in music theory, practice your instrumental techniques, put your heart into your musical expression and deeply hear the sounds you and your fellow musicians are making.

And thus, music *education* should attend equally to all four. Teachers who plan their classes accordingly are qualified to be distinguished members of the prestigious musical 4H Club. Its essential principles:

- **HEARING** is experiencing the world through the senses (here with a music emphasis).
- **HAND** is shaping of the world through doing.
- **HEART** is feeling the world through emotion.
- **HEAD** is understanding the world through thinking.

The Piano Lesson

Remember your piano lessons? Chances are that as a listener, you've experienced music that brought you joy and yet as a beginning player, your music lesson was filled with pain. Even if you were one of the lucky ones who liked your teacher, did well reading notes and ended up playing some reasonably satisfying music, it's likely that you didn't always wholly understand what you were playing or how the piece was put together or why you should get louder here and softer there or how to just play without that piece of paper in front of you. In short, your 4 H's were not wholly engaged.

Your hand, of course, was busy (and with curved fingers —or else!), but rarely did you really understand the music kinesthetically in the whole body, feeling the different weights of each beat in the waltz or using the breath to determine the phrase. Indeed, the commonly accepted strategy of entering the music through reading those black dots on paper put your body to sleep the way that reading tends to do, inhibiting your natural impulse to *move* to music. (Note the difference between the bodies of the churchgoers singing hymns by reading out of a book and the gospel singers who learned by ear.)

Your head was busy translating notated symbols but was not attending to the more crucial issues of understanding patterns, forms, melodic construction and harmonic movement. You could limp or glide through the task of reading the notes and rhythms and pushing the right or wrong keys at the right or wrong times but would be at a loss to improvise from the melody or compose another piece in the style.

Worried about the stern reprimand of the teacher or preoccupied with getting the notes right, it was equally possible for you to play without feeling the beauty in it. The heart needs a safe and relaxed environment before it agrees to open up. Stress, anxiety, worry and fear are the archenemies of the open heart and far too often permeate the atmosphere of the lesson or recital as students are stressed about playing the right notes.

Because the subject here is music whose dominant sense is hearing, we need the fourth H to complete our musical education. Again, because the learning of music through reading uses a visual approach for an aural experience, it reverses the indisputable truth of "sound before symbol. " It makes it possible that music students might not truly hear what they are playing. Naturally, they "hear" it as vibrations that strike their eardrum, but without the whole body experience, the intellectual understanding, the heartfelt connection, they can't wholly hear it in the way it is meant to be heard.

The Orff Class

The Orff approach to music education is a radical antidote to this narrow spectrum of engagement. Music students learning through the Orff approach may eventually come to be proficient music read-ers, but first they will experience music wholly through the body and voice. They will play a wide variety of instruments—xylophones, recorders, drums, bells, shakers and a host of other percussion instruments, training their hands to multiple techniques before settling on one particular instrument. They will be able to play by ear—sing what they play, play what they sing, sing and play at the same time, all the test of true hearing. They will be taught to name the basic concepts used in their playing—rhythms, meters, scales, harmonies, compositional devices—and prove their understanding through improvisation and composition. Finally, though they cannot be instructed to "feel the beauty," they can be led by a teacher who creates a joyful atmosphere and opens the heart to receive the deep emotional messages of music. They will be *enjoying* the making of music.

In the inspired Orff class, music enters the body and the hips respond first (another H!), then the hand shapes a more conscious response, the head analyzes and conceptualizes the key patterns and the heart exults in both the pleasure of the effort and the result of the music. Orff insists on keeping the trio of "Play, Sing and Dance" * in constant company with each other. Dancing trains the body as an instrument of expression, singing opens the heart, playing (especially the keyboard-like xylophones) helps cultivate an intellectual understanding. When you can play what you sing and sing what you dance and dance what you play, you become a musician much larger than someone who can merely decode symbols and press the right keys.

Though the Orff class aims towards these fuller experiences, the Orff teacher will still need a more conscious understanding about what sets the approach apart from business as usual. Here is where the 4H's can help reveal what's needed for greater musicianship. In planning your class, in teaching your class, in reflecting on your class, ask yourself these questions:

1. Can the children *hear* what they're playing, sing what they hear and sing what they play?
2. Can the children *do* what they're doing with a sense of control and mastery, a quality of grace and eloquence? Is their hand being challenged to grow smarter?
3. Can the children *understand* what they're doing beyond parroting back the information that will be on the standardized test?

---

* The title of my book on Orff Schulwerk.

Do they grasp the fundamental principles and ideas? Can they articulate and express them, expand them?

4. Can they *feel* connected to what they're learning? Do they enjoy it? Is there fun in the process of discovery? Does the lesson mean anything to them?

Let's take a look at the role of each of the H's in turn, then return to the 4H Club at the end.

PART I: HEARING:
Hear! Hear! Let's Listen!

> "For listening is the primary musical activity. The musician listens to his own idea before he plays, before he writes. The basis of all musical advance is more comprehensive hearing."
> —SUSANNE K. LANGER [*]

In 1975, the American Orff Schulwerk Association was just seven years old. That year, a parent had donated six Orff instruments to The San Francisco School and the teachers were delighted—only to soon realize that none of them knew how to use them! Since I had taken a college class on Orff Schulwerk, I knew just enough to be hired as their first music teacher. Once classes began, I desperately went back through my ditto-sheet notes from that college class. It's safe to say that "fake it 'till you make it" was my guiding motto of that first year of teaching.

My memory of classes with the older elementary students was that we mostly improvised collectively on the instruments in one glorious jam session. We'd set up the instruments in the pentatonic scale, someone would start playing an idea, another join in and so on until we got tired and started searching for a way to end the piece. There were no tape recorders going, no attempt to write anything down, no thought we would should try to remember the piece to duplicate later on. I never suggested that we vary the meter or change the tempo or try a new scale. We just *played*.

---

[*] Lewis, Richard: *In Praise of Music*; Orion Press, 1963, p. 36

Later in my career, I would joke about it all as a holding action until I figured out what I was doing. But then I came to realize that though, yes, it needed more structure and accountability and deeper understanding, my instincts were sound. For the "jam session" required that we listen to each other's sounds and respond accordingly, a skill that sometimes gets left out of the perfect lesson plan with all its clever steps.

Think about the music classes you were in as a student and the ones you may be teaching now as a teacher. How much real *listening* is going on? Of course, they're hearing sounds, but are they listening to them?

According to Merriam Webster, to listen means:

1. to pay attention to sound
2. to hear something with thoughtful attention; to give consideration
3. to be alert to catch an unexpected sound

Hear, by contrast means: to perceive or to become aware of by the ear. *

True listening in the music class requires that conscious attention to sound, coupled with the ability to respond musically to what's happening musically. One way to test this is to check in at the end and ask, "What did you hear (because you were listening) that could use improvement?" If someone says that they noticed the group was speeding up or that the basses were playing too loud, then you know the class is on the right track.

---

* There can also be a deeper meaning to "hear." In the movie *White Men Can't Jump*, a black man tells his white friend that white men can't hear Jimi Hendrix: "Problem is you're not supposed to listen, you're supposed to hear it. There's a difference between hearing and listening. You're not *hearing* Jimi, you're just listening." If someone says "I hear what you're saying," they mean they really get it. As distinct from "I'm listening to what you're saying." "Hearing" in this sense means listening beyond the notes to the deeper meaning. But as in the dictionary definitions above, hearing can also mean just the physical act of sound striking the ear drum while "listening" means a more conscious attention.

I once attended a recital in which two young students were playing a Mozart violin and piano duet. Somehow, one of them got off and yet they both kept playing their parts a measure apart. Naturally, the lines didn't fit together like this, but they continued on to the end. Playing by reading can put you in a tunnel of sorts, just you, your instrumental part and the written notes and the possibility of playing them without really knowing how they fit with the other parts.

By contrast, the aural approach to teaching tends to demand higher listening skills. But even here, someone can learn their part by rote and play it well, but not attend to how it fits with the other parts. The best test is the invitation to *create* music by layering your sound in with the other sounds. Back to the jam session. Not necessarily the whole class the whole year long. But don't neglect it—it will strengthen those listening muscles in just the way music likes it to.

Finally, ear-training. The ability some people have to hear a song and instantly play it on an instrument appears like a God-given talent to those schooled in paper music, but in fact is a skill like any other that is available to all, easily taught and practiced. Here's a sequence that I use with kids as young as first grade:

1. Echo my solfege patterns. (Do-re-mi/mi-re-do/ do-re-do/ etc.)
2. I'll sing, you echo on xylophone. C=do.
3. I'll sing some patterns again using "la la la." Can you still echo on the xylophone?
4. You sing a small pattern using do-re-mi-sol-la and echo by playing what you sing.
5. You play a pattern and echo by singing what you play.
   Sing and play at the same time, using do-re-mi or loo-loo-loo.

In short, sing what you hear, play what you sing, listen to what you play. Simple, effective and life-changing for the kids in your class. Hear! Hear!

PART II: THE HAND: Hands-on Learning

What is the link between hand and mind? How does the hand shape our character? What is its role in our overall development? Again, our investigation starts with attention to the language we use. Listen to all the expressions that equate the hand with knowledge:

> I know it like the back of my hand. First-hand knowledge. Second-hand information. Hands-on learning. Handbook. Manual. Get a handle on. Grasp the meaning of. Reach for an idea. Be in touch with.

The hand also speaks to us about social relationships. *Hand-in-hand. Take my hand. Shake hands. Talk to the hand. Upper hand. High-handed. Close at hand. Show me your hand (cards). Eating out of my hand. Helping hand. Right- hand man. I've got to hand it to you. Grab attention. Reach out and touch someone.*

Work? *Handy. Handiwork. Ranch hand. All hands on deck. Have a hand in.*

Emotion? *That was a gripping scene. That was touching. That was striking.*

Our daily conversation is peppered with *offhand* remarks that speak a deeper wisdom than what we try to say—*the right hand often doesn't know what the left is doing.* No need to drive this point home with a *heavy hand*—our idioms speak for themselves. *On the other hand,* our understanding of the role of the hand in our development may be *handicapped* if we don't *gather* these expressions, *hold* them up to the light, even *poke* and *prod* them a bit to get them to speak more clearly. It *tickles* my fancy to think that *hands down,* the hand and its associated verbs are everywhere in our talk describing intelligence, character, work and social relations. Whether we're living *hand to* mouth or rising in the world *hand over fist,* the hand and mind are walking side-by-side *holding hands.*

The hand not only has its own form of intelligence, but also shapes our mind, our character and our culture. *How much* we use our hands determines something of mind, *how* we use them reveals character and *what* we do with them creates culture. As such, hands-on learning is not a faddish progressive idea—it is an essential starting point for young children. In conversation with head and heart, it is a vital component of higher education as well. Conversely, trends in education, work and culture that seek to by-pass the hand are a threat to the intelligence of our children.

The Hand in Human Evolution

To begin with the long view. One of many key moments in human evolution came with the development of the opposable thumb. It was our capacity to grip objects that transformed us into toolmakers, allowed us to throw rocks, pound open nuts and dig for roots. Chimps also have thumbs, but their shorter size and lack of flexible rotation allow them to touch only the second and third fingers and not the fourth and fifth as well. That simple distinction severely curtails the stability and flexibility of grip when handling tools.

Less commonly known is the role of upright posture in our evolution. Some 3 or 4 million years ago, the emerging prototype of modern humans was a bi-pedal being, walking on two legs rather than four. Because the hand did not have to support weight, it was free to take on other tasks. Other partners in the evolution of the hand included increased shoulder and pelvic rotation allowing for a more efficient throwing action distinct from our closest primate relatives.

While the hand was developing, what was happening in the brain? Measuring skull cages of our ancestors, we can speculate that Australopithecines had a brain size of 400–500 cc's. Its descendant Homo Habilis brain grew to 600–700 cc's, Homo Erectus, 900–1100 cc's, and Homo Sapiens, appearing around 100,000 years ago, 1,350 cc's, our present brain size. The important point here is that changes in the hand preceded changes in the brain.

Anthropologist Sherwood Washburn speculates that the tripling of brain size between Australopithecines and Homo Sapiens was due in no small part to a million years of tool use. He writes:

"From the short term view, human structure makes human behavior possible. From the evolutionary point of view, behavior and structure form an interesting complex, with each change in one affecting the other." *

In other words, we do what we do because of the way our bodies and brains are constructed. If you change one, you change the other. When bodies begin to do different things, brains change. When brains change, bodies do different things. We needn't speculate from skeletal remains about such processes—we can see them at work everyday in the lives of children and confirmed by neuroscientists. Dr. Kenneth A. Klivington notes that:

"Structure and function are inseparable. We know that environments shape brains; all sorts of experiments have demonstrated that it happens. There are some studies currently being done that show profound difference in the structure of the brain depending on what is taken in by the senses." †

As brains change in response to the environment, so does the environment begin to change from the actions generated by the new brains in a kind of constant dialogue and feedback loop. As the active agent of interaction with the environment, the hand helps build the intelligence of the brain and the brain helps guide the intelligence of the hand.

Another key player in the evolution of Homo Sapiens is the use of language and it is likely that the hand has played (and continues to play) a role here as well. Dr. Frank Wilson wrote:

"Intraspecies cooperation and competition greatly increased the need for an elaborated social structure and communication and for coordinated industry, all of which demanded a more powerful and versatile brain... An emerging language based in the growth of cooperative tool manufacture would have fostered the evolution not only of a more sophisticated tool manufacture but also of a more complex social culture and a more refined language..." ‡

* Wilson, Frank: *The Hand*; Vintage Books, Random House, 1997; p. 16
† Healy, Jane: *Endangered Minds*; Touchstone, Simon & Schuster, 1990: p. 51
‡ Wilson, Frank: *The Hand*; p. 33

The Hand in Child Development

Recalling the evolutionary simultaneity of upright posture, increased hand use and the beginning steps towards language, we can see it all again in each new baby. Why are walking and talking so close to each other? When the one-year old begins walking, the hand is freer to touch and point, enlarging the scope of new things encountered. Close on the heels of increased mobility come the first nouns of recognition—mama, milk, me—each with its own gesture or group of gestures. Once the child can walk to new places, can point and ask "what's that?," the floodgate of language learning opens wide—mobility, gesture and speech develop on near parallel tracks.

Yet the child building language is not simply touching something and naming it. She is feeling it, grabbing it, turning it over, banging it, opening it, throwing it, using the full capacity of the hand to know the object held, to manipulate it and to find out what it can do. In the process, she is building thought, discovering how things relate, how they work, how a sequence of actions function. In building thought, she is building the neural connections in the brain, which includes the capacity of language to store and describe it. The hand is involved every step of the way. It grabs the block (name), then two blocks (number), puts one on top of the other (spatial perception), builds a tower (new name and object created), knocks it down (cause and effect action). As she builds connections between actions, the grammar and syntax of language builds as well. "I build tower." "Tower fall down." As Wilson describes it:

> "The child learns with real objects by trial and error, to make constructions that are inevitably composed as discrete events unified through a series of actions. Playing with anything to make something is always paralleled in cognition by the creation of a story." [*]

Note also how deeply connected hand and speech are in young children. A three-year old simply cannot tell you how old she is

---

[*] Wilson, Frank: *The Hand*; p. 195

without putting up her three fingers simultaneously. When reading kicks in, the hand is reduced to holding the book, but there is no developmental reason why it can't stay connected in conversation. (Consult your nearest Italian to test this truth!) Watch an eloquent speaker and see how the hand leads the thought, punctuates the phrase, accents the idea, emphasizes the point. Articulate speech is a dance between hand and tongue—as they waltz around the floor, they alternately lead and follow.

Maria Montessori's book, *The Absorbent Mind*, based on lectures given in the 1940's, includes an entire chapter titled "Intelligence and the Hand." The practical work that emerged from her observations of children and vision of their development can be seen first-hand in the Montessori schools. These schools are based on creating an environment that not only gives the hands permission and opportunity to explore, but also offers materials that guide the hand towards mastery, articulation and the building of thought. Children in these schools are cutting carrots, tying shoes, finger-painting, fitting together puzzles, laying out rods of different lengths, building towers, matching shapes, tracing sandpaper letters, chiming bells of different pitches and more. Left alone, children will do what nature intended and develop their own unconscious program of development in the woods behind their house. By following the grain of the child's instinct within a school environment, Montessori and other approaches focus and gently guide this work towards greater depth of thought and action. The teacher observes the dialogue between hand and mind and asks the leading questions that enrich them both.

There are other players in the conversation and they include the eye and the ear. Writing, drawing and ball play all require a hand-eye coordination for success. The eye sees the ball in the air, the hand estimates the moment when it should close to catch, the mind notes the success or failure and stores one or strategizes to correct the other. The process is repeated and repeated and repeated until mastery is achieved. This is how we grow the intelligence of the hand, the eye and the brain. The hand grows smarter by adjusting the nuances of time, space, touch and energy, the eye grows keener and the brain stores the information in myelinated pathways that free it to make the next neuron connection.

The same process occurs with hand-ear coordination. The ear hears "squeak" on the recorder, the mind registers "bad," and the fingers adjust to cover the hole. The musical intelligence grows within this feedback loop. A child who only listens to music and never plays with the hand, another who moves her fingers on the piano keys following the dots on paper but doesn't listen clearly, a third who plays and listens but has no theoretical knowledge of what she's doing—none will fully reach the promise of their musical intelligence.

Hand and Character

Contemporary politics notwithstanding, intelligence is still somewhat valued in schools and parents still want their kids to be smart. If you introduce a new idea or revisit an old one into schools or education policy, you better try to sell it by suggesting that it will make us smarter. We play Mozart now to improve our math scores, [*] send our children to Montessori schools so they'll learn to read better, create Maker's Spaces and Tinkering Schools so our kids will invent the next app to make them rich. I do believe that children with extensive informal and formal experiences with hand-work will indeed grow the myriad neuron connections that make them "smart." But there's more to a complete education than the brain's ability to solve problems. An education built on the hand is one that recognizes, builds and reflects character as well.

The very structure of our hand guarantees our individuality, as both FBI agents and palm readers well know. But the kind of character meant here is more than a simple fingerprint or configurations of lines on the palm. It is the way in which different people do the same thing.

---

[*] Research linking music study with improved math performance found that children playing keyboards did better than children just singing—it was the hands' involvement in the process that fed pattern understanding in the brain.

When the hand engages with the world, it encounters the resistance of physical material. Molding a lump of clay, striking a drum, weaving a cloth, massaging a back, throwing a ball, chopping a vegetable, writing with a pen—all offer a wide range of possible touches, pressures, strokes, weights. Five people hitting a gong * or shooting a basket will all have distinct and unique styles. *How* we execute similar tasks will reveal something of our individuality, will bespeak something of our character. It's how we discover what we can do, who we are and what sets us apart.

To take but one example from the world of music: We can recognize the jazz pianists Thelonious Monk and Bill Evans as much by their touch as by their musical ideas. More interesting yet, those ideas are directly related to their touches—Monk's pithy, percussive jabs and Evans' flowing lyrical lines. Which came first? Were the ideas an outgrowth of their natural techniques or the techniques a means of realizing the ideas? Like all the partnerships explored in this chapter, we may never know—but that there exists an ongoing conversation between them is the important point.

It appears that hands not only build brains in general ways, but in quite specific ways as well. That is to say, the digital requirements of the wind instrument as distinct from the guitar, piano, violin and timpani (to name but a few) creates very specific neural pathways that in turn creates distinct nuances of intelligence—and character. Once again, we're in the chicken-egg mire. Does the bassoonist's character develop along certain lines because she plays the bassoon every day or is her personality predisposed to the qualities of the bassoon? Perhaps some things are just best noted and left alone, away from the prodding of neuroscientists and psychologists. Suffice it to say that string players the world over, whether it be on guitars, mandolins or koras, feel a certain affinity for each other, as do drummers, accordionists and bagpipe players. Simply put, they've traveled down similar neural pathways together.

---

* In the Zen Center that I attend, the student must strike a bell before entering the interview with the Zen master. It was claimed that he could tell who was coming and the depth of their meditation by the mere sound of the bell!

Beware the Machine!

Modern American culture, with a long history of fascination with machines and labor-saving devices, a leaning towards ease and comfort, a classist disdain of manual labor, is a conspiracy against the hand. Consider the Cuisinart, the drum machine, the computer mouse, the automatic car wash. Electric doors, electric drills, electric toothbrushes. Automatic garage door openers, automatic flush toilets, automatic transmissions. Dishwashers, dryers, dustbusters. Power saws, power mowers. Pre-torn lettuce, pre-wrapped fruit, pre-sliced bread. In a mere twenty-five years, the hand's role in the task of daily lives has declined dramatically. Gone is the *range* of the hand's actions—dialing a phone, winding a watch, cranking a pencil sharpener, pinching a clothespin, drying a dish, slicing the bread, turning the doorknob, tearing the lettuce, shelling the peas, kneading the dough, grating the cheese, whipping the cream, turning the key in the car door, shifting the gear, returning the typewriter carriage—the variety of hand articulations are reduced to tearing open the package, flicking the switch or pushing the button. Gone is the sensual involvement of pinching fruit, washing dishes, sanding wood, shuffling cards, all the textures of the physical world. Gone is the *nuance* of weight, pressure, angle, force. The entire vocabulary of hand-speech has been drastically decreased. Hands that simply push buttons are dumb in both senses of the word—unable to speak and not as smart as those that work the world.

One might argue that hands are simply doing different things these days—and except for sports, which mostly have stayed the same, that is somewhat true. More children are learning typing skills and some children's marksmanship developed by video games so astounded one ex-Marine that he wrote a book titled, "Stop Teaching Our Children How to Kill." We not only should wonder if kids are as manually intelligent as formerly, but what the impact the contemporary use of the hand has on brain *and* heart development. It is not simply a matter of assuring a concrete foundation for the abstract tasks of later education. How we use our hands impacts character and culture as well, touches on the very soul of humanity. "Beware the machine" means "be aware" of its gifts and limitations, its potentials and its dangers. Montessori said:

> "The hand is in direct connection with man's soul, and not only with the individual's soul, but also with the different ways of life that men have adopted on the earth in different places and at different times. The skill of man's hand is bound up with the development of his mind, and in the light of history we see it connected with the development of civilization. The hands of man express his thought, and from the time of his first appearance upon the earth traces of his handiwork also appear in the records of history." *

I often have done the game, Here We Go 'Round the Mulberry Bush with the kids, with its various verses with accompanying motions: "This is the way we wash the clothes/ chop the fruit/ play the drums/ mail the letter/ milk the cow, " all of the above which now can be done with a push of a button. The grand sweep of the hand's rich vocabulary is reduced to pushing a cold tiny button with one finger or several with two thumbs. What does this mean for the shaping of our children's minds and their pleasurable engagement with the world? What will a future civilization say about us when studying our mass-produced "handiwork?" What will they think when they uncover evidence of brightly-lit Walmarts, thrown-together fast-food joints, Pokemon, Barbie and Disney graphics, shopping malls appendaged to every small town? They will see a culture who traded aesthetics for efficiency, quality for quantity, craft for assembly line, natural materials for plastic, character for comfort, soul for stuff. And the loss of manual dexterity will have had a hand in the decline.

The Arts as Hand Therapy

In the light of the above, the arts are more important than ever to keep children's hands, intelligence and character flowing and flourishing. Visual arts programs not only train the hand to work with

---

* Montessori, Maria: *The Absorbent Mind*; Delta Books, Dell, 1967; p. 150

the eye to see the world, but enlarge its range of motion through painting, weaving, claywork, woodwork, basketry and host of other crafts. P.E. programs will naturally hone different ball skills, but why not also fencing, archery, juggling. And music, particularly in the Orff Schulwerk, emphasizes exposure to an enormous variety of percussion instruments that require a wide spectrum of hand motions—scraping the guiro, shaking the maracas, twisting the afuché, slapping the conga drum, striking the cowbell, playing tremolos on xylophones, fingering the holes on recorders. Musicians are not necessarily "smarter" than non-musicians, but they are smarter in a different way and it's not too far a stretch to consider that using the hand in multiple ways can help pave the way to using the mind in multiple ways.

Here is a rhyme I wrote as a remediation tool for kids to try out the motions their daily life doesn't often demand. Make sure they chant it to a beat and consider some instrumental sound effects with some of the images. Invite the kids to add some of their own verses as well.

The Wisdom of the Hand

Shelling the peas, grating the cheese.
Slicing the bread, making the bed
Kneading the dough, tying the bow
Dialing a phone, pulling meat from a bone.
Drying a dish, cleaning a fish
Turning the key, pouring the tea
Beating the egg, twisting the peg,
Turning the knob, scraping corn from the cob
Hammering the nail, sorting the mail
Winding a clock, giving a knock
Sawing the log, petting the dog
Chopping the wood, opening the hood
Turning the screw, buckling the shoe
Washing the clothes, sorting in rows
Hanging the shirt, digging in dirt
Stirring the soup, scooping the poop.
Packing the bag, wringing the rag
Pulling the weed, stringing the bead
Spraying the can, waving the fan.

Shaping the pot, untying the knot
Sweeping the floor, opening the door,
Raking the leaves, binding the sheaves
Scraping the ice, looking for lice
Shoveling the snow, shooing the crow
Pushing the broom, cleaning the room
Watering the plant, killing the ant
Strumming guitars, driving the cars,
Playing the flute, buttoning the suit.
Tying the tie, zipping the fly
Typing on keys, crossing the t's,
Shaking the drink, wiping the sink
Combing the hair, eating the pear.
Kissing the cat, swinging the bat
Milking the cow, feeding the sow
Shaking the hand, stretching the band
Hugging the friend, Stop! It's the end!

PART III: THE HEAD: Start Making Sense

In the movie *Stop Making Sense*, there is footage of a live concert by the Talking Heads. The band members come out one at a time, so the volume and energy of the music slowly builds until it cranks up full throttle. The band is really in the zone and you can feel the energy in the crowd growing as the music crescendos to an earth-shaking climax. After the last note fades away and the crowd settles a bit, David Byrne takes the microphone and says, "Are there any questions?"

No, there were not. Nobody goes to a rock concert because they want to learn something about music. They want to release themselves fully into the music, either actively dancing in their body or actively listening in their mind. The music and dance are there to get you *out* of your head and *into* your body and your heart, to *stop making sense* and start feeling sensual. At the end of the rock concert, no one cares about asking whether that was the IV chord the guitarist changed to in bar 5. The experience is all. Music education is often just learning *about*, music concerts are the thing itself.

By advocating here that music education be more musical, feel more like a concert than a lecture, there is a danger of being misunderstood. A casual observer watching kids in a class dancing freely to scarves or jamming on the Orff instruments might be concerned that it feels just a bit too much like a party to be a genuine school subject. "Sure, the kids are having fun, but are they *learning* anything?" Or to translate to the language of education: "Are the kids *aware* of what they're learning and able to group and re-group their experiences into clear, useful and understandable concepts?"

And the answer is, "No. Not unless you lead them from that next step from the body to the mind, from the experience to the concept." That's your job as a music educator—to help the students *start to make sense* of what they just experienced. However, for it to be fully effective, you'll need to take a different route than simply defining a concept:

> "The beat is a regular pulsation with constant intervals between each pulsation."

What does that mean to a student who has just walked into class? Nothing more than another factoid to memorize and promptly forget. Consider this alternative approach to learning the concept of beat with first graders:

> "What did you have for breakfast this morning? (students share). Well, last week I had oatmeal and sometimes people call oatmeal porridge. Do you know this rhyme?
>
> 'Pease porridge hot, pease porridge cold
>
> Pease porridge in the pot, nine days old.'
>
> Can you pat your knees while you recite? Can you clap the words while you recite? Can you find a place to put in two snaps when your voice stops?

After practicing the above in a variety of ways, now's the time to name each of these experiences and make conscious the function of each.

> "Note that we patted a steady sound on our knees. When our voices stopped at the end of the line, the sound kept going. This is called the beat. We can find it in our body and mostly

> it is regular. If we run, it can get faster, if we sleep, it can get slower, but it always returns to a regular steady pulse. Almost all music has the beat to tie everything together.
>
> "When we clap the way the words sound, that's called the *rhythm* and it's different from the *beat*. If there's music that doesn't have words, the rhythm is the way the words would sound if there were words. Because it changes and has some moments when it stops, it's what makes the music interesting.
>
> "Those snaps we put in the spaces between the words? That's called a *color* part. It's like a little bit of salt or spice added to make everything more tasty, like a little splash of color in a black-and-white drawing.
>
> I'm going to play something and tell me if it's the beat, rhythm or color."

So far, so good. This is school all the way. The kids are learning a concrete concept, they're responsible for identifying it in a variety of contexts, they're accountable for remembering it and yes, it will be on the test. The kids are happy to increase their vocabulary and for extra credit, they can learn to spell the words ("rhythm" just might win them the Spelling Bee some day!).

But in the large picture of music-making, we might say, "So what?" How does this really contribute to their making of music, to their enjoyment, to their deep understanding?

To complete the process, the children must create something new from what they've just learned. This both reveals their understanding and generates some satisfying music.

- Invite the kids to find three percussion instruments. One will play the beat, one the rhythm of the Pease Porridge rhyme, one the color part.
- Decide which instrument will play which and play the poem twice.
- Then switch—a different instrument plays the color, a different one the rhythm, a different one the beat.

- Switch again. Decide which they prefer or use all combinations in a set sequence.
- Share.

Armed with the knowledge of how these three concepts work, clear about the words that describe them, the kids now have the power to instantly create music. Instead of you having to describe each time, "Now one of you play a steady pulsing at regular intervals, another play a combination of short and long duration values with occasional rests, another search for the rests in the second and fill them in with a short little phrase, you can simply say, "You play the **beat**, you play the **rhythm**, you play the **color**. Go!"

This is the power of conscious conceptual knowledge. Experiences are gathered under the umbrella of a single word or phrase, condensed into an efficient container that allows you to store them and group them. The single word "meter," for example, accounts for all the ways you can group beats, the different weights and accents the beats might have, the different associated motions or dance steps, the different ways it houses rhythmic and melodic phrases. Once you understand that word, you now have the power to quickly access this musical element, call it up and put it to use, expand it back out again to its multiple facets. Contract it with a named concept, expand it with a musical action. It's efficient, effective and helps you do something more quickly and more clearly. It's helpful to analyze music you're hearing and it's helpful for you to compose music. By fifth grade, you can send a group off and say, "Come back with a piece in Dorian mode, 5/4 meter, slow tempo." Whereas the non-trained musician will say "Huh?!", the kids trained to marry conceptual understanding with their intuitive aural explorations will say, "Got it! See you in five!"

It also houses variations within a single idea. You can play the beat with different hand combinations, on different parts of your body, on different instruments, at different tempos, with different dynamics and energy. You can move to the beat, you can express it in gestures without sound, you can draw the beat, you can arrange blocks to look like the beat, you can look around the room and see what looks like the beat—windows, ceiling tiles, a row of overhead lights. We might notice it in crows perched on a wire or hear it in the sound of the frog or the chirp of the cricket. * Following our "one thing one hundred ways" idea, this single concept then is experienced and explored in multiple dimensions with the unifying thread of constant impulses at regular intervals.

Humans seem to be the only creatures who are cognizant of what they know. We all have an intuitive understanding of how to navigate through the world, but it is the conscious understanding, the ability to name, identify, articulate, expand what we know that sets us apart from other corners of creation. To master any field of study requires a deep understanding of a special set of knowledges, with its particular vocabulary, working ideas and key concepts. In music, like other fields, there is no sidestepping the role of the mind, but in the end, such knowledge is never an end in itself, but invisibly stitched into the playing of the music. When we listen to John Coltrane, we are wholly brought into the power of his saxophone without considering how he used Dorian, melodic minor, pentatonic and chromatic scales improvising over the E minor 7 chord. He himself was certainly not thinking in his head while soloing, "Okay, start with Dorian and throw in that pentatonic riff and then switch to melodic minor." All the theory work and practice he did before the gig was embedded in the mind, ear and fingers and sewn into the spontaneous moment. But if you asked him, he could tell you about those scales.

In short, the *head* is a necessary and powerful partner in the *hand* and *hearing* trio, but always in service to the music itself. And there is yet one more player in the group.

---

* Poet Gary Snyder noticed the different beats of the natural world in this gem of a poem:

> As the cricket's soft autumn hum is to us,
> so are we to the trees
> as are they
> to the rocks and the hills.

Snyder, Gary: *Axe Handles*, North Point Press, 1983, p.51

PART IV: THE HEART: Playing by Heart

"The joy of the heart begets song."
—The Talmud [*]

"Music rises from the human heart. When the emotions are touched, they are expressed in sounds, and when the sounds take definite forms, we have music."
—Confucius [†]

"Gladden thine heart, drum thine drum and pipe thine pipe"
—Arabian Nights [‡]

"Music appeals to the heart, whereas writing is addressed to the intellect; it communicates ideas directly, like perfume."
—Honoré de Balzac [§]

"Music represents the inner feeling in the exterior air and expresses what precedes, accompanies or follows all verbal utterance."
—Wilhelm Heinse [¶]

Isn't it interesting that when classically trained musicians memorize the music and put down the paper, it's called "playing by heart?" It's as if admitting that the tunnel vision of reading a score runs the danger of shutting out the heart. When you finally put the paper aside, you can release yourself more fully to your expressive playing and let the heart speak.

I've put the heart last in the 4H club, but when it comes to music, it always has both the first and the last word. Music can animate the body, challenge the intellect, engage the senses, but the beginning and end of the matter is how it touches the heart. Music is the language of emotion, the one that can express more precisely, coherently, unequivocally what we are feeling than anything else. Here's how the composer Felix Mendelssohn talks about it:

---

[*] Lewis, Richard: *In Praise of Music*; p. 3
[†] Ibid.; p. 6
[‡] Ibid.; p. 12
[§] Ibid.; p. 23
[¶] Ibid.; p. 24

"People often complain that music is too ambiguous; that what they should think when they hear it is so unclear, whereas everyone understands words. With me it is exactly the reverse, and not only with regard to an entire speech, but also with individual words. These, too, seem to me so ambiguous, so vague, so easily misunderstood in comparison with genuine music, which fills the soul with a thousand things better than words." *

Another composer, Roger Sessions, says a similar thing:

"Emotion is specific, individual and conscious; music goes deeper than this, to the energies which animate our psychic life, and out of these creates a pattern which has an existence, laws and human significance of its own. It reproduces for us the most intimate essence, the tempo and the energy of our spiritual being, our tranquility and our restlessness, our animation and our discouragement, our vitality and our weakness—all, in fact, of the fine shades of dynamic variation of our inner life. It reproduces these **far more directly and more specifically** than is possible through any other medium of human communication. (boldface mine). †

If emotion is at the deep center of music, the prize at the end of the labyrinth walked with hand, head and hearing, shouldn't we account for it in the music classroom? Shouldn't it be something as important to assess as a physical technique or an understood concept?

Shouldn't we take care to create an atmosphere in which the full range of emotion is invited to blossom?

This has long been the ultimate cognitive dissonance of music class. That music, one of life's most joyous experiences, can be one of school's most painful classes, makes exactly no sense whatsoever. How can one teach music honestly or effectively without bringing the emotion the music is designed to bring forth into the atmosphere of the class? And yet far too often, we find bored kids fooling around in music class with a perpetually stressed angry teacher yelling at the kids, "Hey, if I see that one more time, I'm cancelling the concert!!

---

* Lewis, Richard: *In Praise of Music*; p. 68
† Ibid.; p. 76

Now the audience is counting on us to bring them some joy in this dismal world, so let's get to work and SING WITH JOY, DAMN-IT!!! I said, JOY!!!" I, for one, have never found that command to work.

Naturally, there is no formula for bringing joy into the classroom. The best one can do is to enter each class with your own joy intact, your pleasure in teaching palpable, your love of music manifest, your enthusiasm and excitement for what you have to offer infectious. Emotion, like music, is a vibration passed on below the belt of verbal directions or commands. Joy begets joy, laughter releases laughter, tears precipitate tears, anger unleashes anger or fear. The first job of any teacher is to come into each class filled with love for your work, love for your subject, love for your students.

If you're going to play music, why then, *please* play music in the playful way that children best learn. Yes, there is serious work and rigorous study involved, but once you set a playful tone, you give permission for emotion to bloom, for the heart to be gladdened in the way that music suggests.

And then please observe the children. You can't assess emotion as you can facts or techniques, but it doesn't mean it's beyond assessment. Just *watch* them. If they say at the end of an activity, "Can we do it again?" or at the end of the class "Aww! Do we have to go to recess? This is more fun than recess!" you're on the right track. If you see them in some kind of tranquil trance-state while playing the drone on the bass xylophone, you're doing well. If you feel the room lit up by their energy and laughter, it's a sign that things are on the right track. If you ask how many enjoyed what they just did and 100% hands shoot up explosively, that's good feedback. If a parent tells you that their kid didn't want to go to school and then changed her mind when she realized she had music class today, you can go to sleep peacefully at night. If you come in to Pre-school Singing Time and the kids shout out your name and start joyfully chanting it, you know that you're in the right job. All of the above has happened in my classes and has helped me understand that my efforts to get better at my job bore fruit because it helped make a child's day just a little bit happier. And that now both the children and I have the tools to tell about that happiness through music.

The 4H Partnership

Look again at the traditional piano lessons through the 4H lens. Learning and playing by deciphering the notes on paper means never being asked to truly *hear* what you're playing, never being asked to sing what you play and play what you sing. Never being asked to *understand* how Bach put this little song together and show how you can transpose it if you understand its structure, how you can compose a similar piece following its chord progression. Never being asked how you *feel* about the piece. Stumbling in broken rhythms through figuring out the written notes, practicing one measure over and over, taking a long time in each piece to actually feel the music of it. Never being asked to move the phrase in the whole body to feel the different weights within the meter or show the direction and energy of the phrase so that your hand can do it all better when you sit back down at the piano.

Look again at traditional music education through the 4H lens. In college, you might take a music theory class that is head only, sing in a gospel choir that runs on heart, take lessons that focus on technique or take an ear-training class, but you see how we specialize and tear apart that which belongs together. Every musical class at any age should light up each of these faculties and in the order (but not always) suggested. And at the end, they all move from the conscious back to the intuitive in the final performance, buried (but still alive) deep in the heart of the act of music-making. Having passed wholly through the hand, head, heart and hearing, the music will sing out more fully. And isn't that the point of music education?

The 4H's in the School Curriculum

Do these ideas apply to other subjects as well? I believe they do. Other fields will demand some kind of sensory intelligence beyond following directions. As we've noted, when we enter music primarily through decoding symbols, we don't let *hearing* guide us through the venture. If we cook wholly from following directions in the recipe book, we might miss the important piece of constantly adjusting by *tasting* our cooking. If we treat art like a paint-by-number activity, we bypass deep *seeing*. If we are sanding wood according to some formula of the correct number of sandpaper strokes, we don't attend fully enough to *touch*. If we are concocting perfume in a lab, we would do well to trust our sense of *smell* more than the given formula. In short, the *senses* need to be wholly invited to work together with systems and symbols and procedures and formulas.

Not all subjects marry the *body* to the mind in the way that the arts do. But some will require the intelligence of the hand—dentistry, surgery, massage, carpentry, car mechanics and such. And even the more abstract heady subjects will find some bodily involvement as the math teacher shapes ideas with his or her hands while teaching or the poet dances the words to bring them fully alive.

We are only just beginning to understand how essential the *heart* is to learning, how our feeling about the learning affects how deeply it's imbedded and where and for how long. If a particular piece of learning came from a place of trauma—even if it be as small as a teacher shaming you in front of a class or anxiety while studying for the test—the emotional memory will prefer not to revisit that trauma and bury the learning. If by contrast, it is associated with joy and a loving welcome, well, wouldn't we all like to go back time and again to that room? So all teachers will do well to consider how joy enters their curricular plans.

Finally, the *head* is at the center of much of school's mission, but to actually engage the whole of the brain requires something more than mere imitation and fact gathering. All of the body's faculties have a second room somewhere in the brain and for the mind to reach full throttle, the inclusion of the hand, heart and senses will be needed.

Postscript

The original 4H Club began in the U.S. around 1902, with the goal of connecting public school education to the practical skills of rural farming. Through the many changes of time and place, it continues to be an active youth organization. Its motto is **Learn to Do by Doing** and its pledge is:

> I pledge my Head to clearer thinking.
> my Heart to greater loyalty.
> my Hands to greater service.
> my Health to better living.
> For my Club, my Community and my Country.

Would that schools adopt such a worthy mission statement! And music teachers. "Learn to Do By Doing" holds true and the pledges, with some slight modifications, also would serve to revitalize music education as we know it:

> I pledge my Head to clearer thinking.
> my Heart to greater feeling.
> my Hands to greater playing.
> my Hearing to better listening.
> For my Band, my Community and the World.
> Anyone want to join?

SUMMARY

HEARING: Create classes in which students must actively listen, show what they can hear, respond to what they hear.

HAND: Develop the intelligence of the hand, each activity introducing, reinforcing or expanding the hand's expressive ability.

HEAD: Develop the ability to understand the unifying concepts behind each piece or music-making activity, to identify, name, describe, expand the key ideas.

HEART: Attend to the joy in your class, note and feed the children's excitement, enthusiasm, enjoyment.

4H Club: Work to keep all four faculties in conversation with each other in every class.

———————————

ACTION: Make a lesson plan designed to expand the hand's technique, the mind's understanding, the heart's feeling and the ear's capacity to hear (or eye to see, nose to smell, mouth to taste). Make conscious each of the above learnings with the students.

REPETITION
REPETITION
REPETITION

CHAPTER 5: ONE THING ONE HUNDRED WAYS: Repetition and Variation

The Art of Repetition

"Do it again!" implores the child. We've long ago tired of playing a game with the toddler and are anxious to check our e-mail. But the child is begging us "Again! Again!" When children want us to tell the same bedtime story again or sing the same song or keep playing catch long past dinnertime, they are speaking an unconscious need for one of the brain's most intriguing strategies to embed learning— *myelination*.

The brain's job is to make sense of experience and in every moment of encounter with the world, send signals from one part of the brain to another, leaping from axon to dendrite. Experiences that repeat catch the brain's attention—"This is important." The face of the mother who gives us food or the face of the neighbor's snarling dog who frightens us signal to the brain that we would do well to remember them more than the random people passing by in the street. Such important information needs a different kind of signal transfer. And that's where myelin comes into play.

The scientific explanation goes like this: When a circuit is repeatedly fired, special cells called oligodendrocytes wrap the nerve with a fatty substance known as myelin. With more repetitions, the myelin thickens until it has become a strong protective sheath that allows the signals to fire more smoothly and rapidly. It's parallel to deciding to pave a dirt road with asphalt once you're convinced that the house at the other end is an important destination. When all the connections necessary to a skill or knowledge, whether motor or cognitive, are fully myelinated, we arrive at an unconscious competence, a dependable, lasting and thoroughly known learning. By insulating the nerve fibers of the axon and allowing impulses to move faster and more efficiently, the brain is now free to pay attention to new connections. The key factor in building the competence? Repetition.

The classic example, which parents of teenagers know so well, is learning to drive. In that first lesson, the new drivers grip the wheel, glue their eyes to the road and pay attention as if their life depended on it—and it does! If the parent asks, "How are you doing, dear?" the answer might be a short and sharp "Don't talk to me!!" A week or so later, they might answer, "Fine." Another week: "Pretty good. Say, what's for dinner tonight?" Within a month or so, they're driving with one hand, turning on the radio, turning around to talk to their friends in the back seat. (By this time, the parent is safely tucked away in the house.)

What happened? Driving became myelinated, became automatic, required less attention. Without the need to concentrate on actions that now are imbedded and somewhat routine, the mind is free to attend to other things.

Intelligence doesn't grow from creating more brain cells—and the one with the most brain cells wins. We are all born with about the same number—somewhere around 100 billion, not counting glial cells. Intelligence is born from making connections between these brain cells and connections are made by repeated experience.

We have known this for some time now, but haven't wholly adjusted our teaching to fit our knowledge. What are the implications for the daily work in the classroom?

Repetition, Repetition, Repetition

Note the word "repetition." Re-petition means to petition the gods again for your wish. In ancient Greece, prayer meant petitioning a specific god who handled your area of concern—fertility, victory, good health, wisdom, what have you. As the religious folks in any faith know, one doesn't just pray once, but over and over again. Physical—and mental—practice demands repetition, a constant act of faith re-petitioning, but not with bowed head and clasped hands. The fingers must find the right paths of notes on the instruments, the feet must follow the steps, the mind must take its practiced powers through disciplined habits of thought, again and again and again.

But how much repetition is enough for sufficient myelination and mastery? A quick survey through Google reveals different opinions—some say 30 to 50 times, some, 300 times, some 3,000 times and yet others, 40,000 times! * Naturally, it's useful to distinguish between chopping a carrot and playing "The Flight of the Bumblebee" on violin. The more complex the task, the more connections will require myelination.

Once connections are myelinated, repeated practice is necessary to keep it going and reinforce the connection. Think of continued practice as a kind of synaptic jumping jacks, re-charging the connections and warming up the body/mind. Like a musician losing calluses on his fingers or chops on his trumpet, we lose ground if we don't keep up our practice. But when we return to it, we can access it much faster having once known it. Again, this varies depending on the complexity of the task. Once we learn to ride a bike, we can return to it after five years away and pretty much remember how to do it. If we try to pick up speaking Spanish after five years away, it

---

* In his book *The Talent Code*, Daniel Coyle suggests that 10,000 hours is the minimum required to master a complex task like brain surgery or Orff Schulwerk teaching.

takes us a while to get up to speed again. But the connections are there, ready to be re-awakened.

One of a thousand mistakes that teachers can make is not giving the children sufficient repetition in a skill or concept. The kids do the puzzle once and we think they have got it. The teacher does a few classes of ball-bouncing skills, a few of soccer kicks, a few of badminton and at the end, little progress is made in any of the three. The teacher asks "Who went to Julliard Conservatory and then dropped out to study at the University of Charlie Parker and Dizzy Gillespie?" and the hands shoot up enthusiastically with the answer ready, "Miles Davis!" Two weeks later, the teacher tells the students about the groundbreaking recording *Kind of Blue* album that Miles Davis made and they say, "Who?"

This problem is true at any age. We need help from our computer-savvy friend and he shows us, "Just press this, then this, then this and Voila! there it is!" "Can you show me that again?" we beg, nodding our head in apparent understanding, jotting down a few notes. The next day, off we go and … "Hmmm. Why isn't this working?" If we do that procedure every day for two weeks, it starts to feel comfortable—myelination at work.

Contemporary teachers and students are particularly vulnerable to falling short on repetition because so many machines are doing work for us. Why sit and chop vegetables for twenty minutes? Throw them in the Cuisinart. Kneel on the ground and pull weed after weed? No thanks, I'll get out the weedwhacker. Add up this whole list of numbers? Where's my calculator? Practice paradiddles on the snare drum? Too much trouble—I'll just turn on the drum machine.

Repetition as a shared practice and honored value has gone down several notches in contemporary culture. We prefer instant success and avoid like the plague anything that might be called "boring." When it comes to education, we're nervous about anything that might seem like the "drill and kill" approach.

And yet the modern child needs the same amount of repetition that his or her 19th century or 9th century or cave-dwelling counterpart did. Culture may change quickly, but brains change slowly. Indeed, as many neuroscientists have discovered, our bodies and brains evolved to meet the needs of conditions some five or even fifty thousand years ago. If our present environment is going to create new evolutionary adaptations, we won't see it in our descendants for at least a few hundred, if not a few thousand, years. There's no rushing evolution and natural selection. That means we have to pay attention to the brains and bodies we have, not imagine that today's generation can sidestep the neural firings that have been going on in our brains for millennia just because they have Gameboy.

Practice and Intelligence

How often have you felt frustrated because you can't do something that your friends can? They can juggle and you can't, they write evocatively and your prose feels wooden, they can multiply numbers in their head and you always have to reach for your calculator. Chances are your self-esteem drops a few feet and you feel that you're not smart or capable. And you might feel that your teacher agrees.

When adult teachers in my workshops are struggling with a challenging task like a tricky body percussion pattern, they find it liberating when I remind them:

> "If you're feeling frustrated and tied-up in self-doubt, wondering 'Why can't I do this?' the answer is simple. 'Because you've rarely or never slapped your body in these kinds of ways before. You're not stupid or uncoordinated—your brain is simply encountering novel information for which it has no previous map. Like me trying to speak a sentence in Thai with sounds I've never heard before and microtonal inflections I've never heard spoken. The good news is that should you care to improve, you will, simply by repeated experience."

If we deeply understand the implications of intelligence as a practice, we can finally be liberated from our doubts about our learning challenges. We will improve in the things we practice and we will practice the things we care about knowing and mastering.

The question is not "Are we smart?" but "what do we care to be smart in?" And "how much work are we willing to put into it?"

This is a unique human dilemma. One horse may run a bit faster than another and one dog may be more affectionate than another, but most animals in the same species equally master what they need for survival. But because of the greater number of brain connections possible in humans, the range of possible skills and knowledges is astronomical in number. No one can be equally smart in all areas. The virtuoso musician who is a championship basketball player and wins the Noble Prize in physics after writing the Great American Novel does not exist and never will.

Part of the grand adventure of life is to discover precisely which of our multiple intelligences is singing out the strongest in the vast choir of possibilities. We note that we might have a knack for taking apart radios and putting them together or find ourselves noticing mathematical pattern in everything we see and touch or hear songs in our head begging to be released and shared. These are things we should pay attention to, whispers from our particular form of genius about what we were put on this earth to pursue. And then comes—practice, practice, practice.

School can be a place to sample multiple possibilities and help children discover where their inclination lies. This does not mean excusing them from math class because they would rather spend their time dancing hip-hop. All intelligences are intimately bound together so that dance will call on logical-mathematical, visual-spatial, musical, linguistic and more intelligences to fully realize its possibility. It's important in the early years to encourage children to persevere in each subject, whether it comes easily or is fraught with challenge.

At the same time, it doesn't make sense to expect children to be equally intelligent in all subjects. As adults, we get to pick and choose. Instead of being shuffled off to learning specialists because we can't fix the car or compose a four-part fugue, we happily hire the mechanic and pay money for the concert ticket, proclaiming, "I choose not to myelinate those particular connections in my brain."

So to repeat yet again: Repetition is essential to education. What the child is saying with "Do it again!" is "I'm not myelinated yet. We have to keep going until the synaptic road gets paved." This is one of the central tenets of what is called "growth mindset," the idea that education is an ever changing verb and it is up to us to improve through our effort. The new mantra is "I can't do this—yet."

Good Practice

That practice reaps progress is indisputable. Yet practice and repetition alone may not be enough to feel wholly successful. There is the question of what *kind* of practice we engage in. We need to distinguish between good practice—that which utilizes the most efficient technique or tried-and-true systematic thinking—and sloppy practice. Good practice requires patience in mastering details, knowing precisely what needs work and taking the time to attend to it. By contrast, some people may put in the same number of hours of piano practice, but rush through or skip over the hard passages or neglect taking time to get the most efficient fingering. Such practice can myelinate a connection in a way that actually hinders our development, creates a lifelong bad habit difficult to break. (I am a victim of my own childhood sloppy piano practice and it's not a pretty sight—or sound!) In short, the *quantity* of practice alone is not useful without the quality of practice.

Some of the effectiveness of good practice has to do with the quality of attention. Is there a sense of preparation beforehand? An anticipation of the task ahead, a living of it first in the imagination? Is there a resonance afterward? An echo that keeps sounding, ideas that keep churning, fingers that continue to practice the technique? The person immersed in this kind of before-during-after practice will naturally have a deeper penetration than the one who just shows up and departs with no anticipation or afterthought.

Then there's the question of emotion. Practice done with enjoyment and pleasure is different than the same done with resentment or stress. *How* we feel about the thing we are doing becomes an inextricable part of what we can accomplish. It feeds our motivation to continue, to work through the hard parts, to develop the willpower that will see us through the boring moments and help us over the hurdles of frustration and self-doubt.

It's tempting to hope some scientist can simply give us a number—"Do this x number of times and you'll get 800 in all SAT scores/ build a better mousetrap / get to Carnegie Hall." But learning is too complex to be reduced to simple formulas. The unique contours of each task, the guidance we receive from teachers who have traveled further down the path, the quality of the practice and our feeling about it all combine to make a one-of-a-kind fingerprint in pursuit of mastery.

For our students to reap the benefits of repetition, we should take care to:

- Give **sufficient time** for the students to practice.
- Model **correct physical techniques** and **thinking routines.**
- Create an atmosphere of joyful pursuit of knowledge—**practice as fun**, not drill.
- Give the **affirmation and encouragement** every learner needs.
- Give the equally **necessary corrections** and **further challenges.**
- Temper the repetition with small **variations within** the repetition (more on this soon)

And so to repeat again. Repetition is an essential strategy at all levels of education and in all subjects. However, there is a timing to it all and a moment when something else is needed. Remember the child asking us to tell the same bedtime story? As we've noted, this is more than comfort food for the soul. It is the brain absorbing at its own pace and rate the essential patterns, images and lessons of the story. And then one night, we begin "Once upon a time, there were three bears…" and the child says, "That story again? Tell me a new one." And that translates to "Myelination complete. Seeking new connections."

The Art of Variation

Here's where the brain's other deep necessity comes into play—novelty. If the brain needs and thrives on repetition to thoroughly embed lifelong learnings, it also is constantly seeking the next novelty to keep growing and developing new connections.

When a learning is first heading toward myelination, all is excitement and pleasure in the journey. But when the learning is firmly established and no new inputs are happening, things start to feel merely routine. The musical groove that once gave us life has become a pounding mechanical disco beat that saps our energy. How to keep these two qualities of the brain—repetition and variation, familiarity and novelty—in constant conversation with each other? And what is the proper ratio between the two?

Remember those 100 billion brain cells waiting for connection? They all require new experiences, constant variation, novel situations, to get wired up. Language is a perfect example of the endless variation that keeps the brain growing—i.e., connecting—because the combinations of a finite number of words are virtually infinite. The baby beginning with "Mama! No! Food!" who arrives as an adult at *"To be or not to be: that is the question: Whether 'tis nobler in the mind to suffer the slings and arrows of outrageous fortune…"* means a lot of connections have been slowly built through the constant interplay of repetition and variation.

Most animals have their movements, sounds, behaviors, instinctually pre-ordained. You can read Shakespeare out loud to your dog hour after hour and he is not going to grow up any differently than his neighbor dog chasing sticks. But humans must cultivate their behavior and intelligence, their speech and their music, their movement and their emotions, through experience. They must earn them. That is the business of education in all its many faces—in the home, the neighborhood, the school, the culture.

Repetition, Repetition, Repetition, Variation

If both repetition and variation are necessary for the brain to develop, the question remains as to how much of each? It would be nice to extrapolate a fool-proof formula applicable to all situations, but like most truths in this world, the best we can do is to treat these formulas as guidelines, not hard-and-fast rules.

One place to look is the various structures we tend towards in our life and art. The most common of these that I have found is the three-to-one ratio. Consider these examples:

> Where oh where is little Dougie? (3x)
> Way down yonder in the paw-paw patch.
>
> Shoo fly, don't bother me. (3x)
> For I belong to somebody.
>
> Polly put the kettle on (3x)
> We'll all have tea.
>
> A little red wagon painted blue (3x)
> Skip to my lou, my darling.
>
> "Someone's been eating my porridge." said the Papa bear.
> "Someone's been eating my porridge," said the Mama bear.
> "Someone's been eating my porridge," said the Baby bear.
> "And she ate it ALL UP!"
>
> Awake in the morning
> Awake in the afternoon
> Awake in the evening
> SLEEP!

ONE THING ONE HUNDRED WAYS:
Repetition through Variation

Asked to comment on her experience in my classes, a teacher once said; **"Instead of doing a hundred things one way, you do one thing a hundred ways."** She noted how we could start with a rhyme, a song, a game or an idea, develop it through variation after variation and experience it through a multitude of mediums. We learn a rhythm pattern and then play it slow, fast, loud, soft, with high sounds, then low sounds. We play it on our bodies, vocalize it with our voice, put words to it, sing it, dance it, play it on percussion instruments, create a melody from it. We might also create counter-rhythms or a second phrase or combine the various media into a coherent composition and choreography. This way of teaching brings the imagination into play, always a great strategy for student involvement and engagement, while offering a thorough investigation of the possibilities of a single simple pattern.

So much of schooling is the opposite—one hundred things one way. Take out your math textbook and turn to page 3. Take out your language arts book and turn to page 4. Take out your history book and turn to page 5. Take out your music book and play the piece on page 6. Now the worksheet, now the homework, finally the test. And now the textbook, worksheet, exam is replaced by the computer—scroll to this Website on your iPad.

Doing one thing one hundred (or five or ten) ways gives the children the best of both worlds—the repetition they need to embed the learning and the variation they need to keep it fresh, interesting and developing. **Variation *within* repetition** is the useful mantra that will change your teaching. You are now prepared to guide your students through a Pedagogy of Possibility, helping them experience the subject at hand from multiple angles and multiple perspectives through multiple senses and multiple intelligences. Apply this practice of variation to any field and watch how your lessons will flower:

- Dribble the basketball with your right hand. Left. Two of each. One of each. Between your legs. Behind your back. While running. Forwards, Backwards. Sideways.
- Paint five still life's, each from a different angle, or in a different style.
- Create five different math word problems that arrive at the same answer.
- Do the same scene from Hamlet using different emotional affects. (Happy Hamlet, bored Hamlet, whiny Hamlet, Hamlet in love, etc.)

- Describe this historical incident from different point of views—the conquerors, the conquered, the bystanders, the ancestors, the descendants.
- Write a poem with the same ideas and images in different styles—haiku, sonnet, ballad, cinquain. sestina.
- Play Bach's Minuet in G in the key of E♭. In minor scale. In 5/4 time. With melody in the left hand. In jazz block chords with swing rhythm.

Now we have a form of repetition that folds in variation and gives us something more than merely memorizing times-tables, practicing our scales and doing the lay-up drills (without wholly replacing these necessary steps). It invites us to see something from multiple angles, to widen our perspective, bring depth to our knowledge and raise our understanding.

This conscious manipulation through variation of a given craft is a tried-and-true artistic practice—think of Hokusai's paintings *36 Views of Mt. Fuji,* Wallace Stevens' poem *Thirteen Ways of Looking at a Blackbird,* Bach's *Goldberg Variations*, all the jazz tunes based on *I Got Rhythm*, the permutations of coffee you can order at Starbucks. Equally as important as these finished examples is the discipline of constant exercise—the jazz musician working out melodic permutations over a II–V–I chord progression, the painter painting model after model. An artful approach to education pays attention to how artists actually develop in their fields.

The above all speak to variations *within* a field, but variation *across* disciplines also gives us a more rounded and thorough understanding. I gave my eighth graders the task of presenting something about Ella Fitzgerald in a medium of their choice. In order to achieve that, they first had to study her life, listen to her music, watch videos, find photographs—the kind of research schools traditionally teach students to do. But each student then spent a special kind of time with Ella as they painted her picture or made a short film or created a game or wrote a poem.

In short, by suggesting, offering or inviting small variations within the repetitions, the students get the best of both worlds—the comfort of the familiar and the excitement of the new, the practice of the repetition and the exploration of the variation, the growing acquaintance with the known and the new possibilities of the unknown. *Repetition through variation* can transform your teaching, modeling for your students a way of learning that can serve them their whole life. They will show you both the satisfied nod of understanding and the excited twinkle of discovery.

Throughout these pages, the details of applying new findings about how the brain functions to the classroom keep pointing to the same place—an *artistic* approach to teaching where play and work join to aid creation, a creation born from repetition and fed by variation. That creation need not always be a work of art per se. It can take the form of a scientific discovery or an experimental recipe. All creative acts keep our brains active and engaged, alert and growing. They move knowledge forward and get us up in the morning eager to find out what the next day has in store for us.

All it takes is a simple question: "How else can we do this?"

SUMMARY

REPETITION
- Repetition is the brain's way to make and keep connections.
- Myelination makes these connections more efficient.
- Continued practice and exercise protects them from synaptic pruning.
- Good practice is better than sloppy practice.
- We are often not good at the things we don't habitually do.

VARIATION
- Novelty is the way the brain creates new connections.
- Variation feeds plasticity and flexibility.
- Multiple points of view help grow intelligence.

REPETITION AND VARIATION
- Repetition without variation is boring and stultifying.
- Variation without sufficient repetition cannot express itself fully.
- The brain needs both repetition and variation.
- The balance leans toward repetition—a a a b.

REPETITION THROUGH VARIATION
- One thing one hundred ways: a win-win for the brain, offering both disciplined practice and creative novelty at once.

ACTION: Take a simple activity (as in partner-clapping game like *Miss Mary Mack*) and come up with 25 variations. When you run out of idea, ask the children: "How else can we do this?"

CHAPTER 6—SIX GUIDELINES FOR DEVELOPING MATERIAL

1. **Simple to Complex**
2. **Body to Instrument**
3. **Unison to Orchestra**
4. **Imitation to Creation**
5. **Aural to Written**
6. **Experience to Concept**

The room was filled with the frustrated groans and grunts of fourth graders trying—with great difficulty—to get their Science Fair projects ready for that evening's presentation. Guitar in hand, I spontaneously started to sing:

"The Science Fair was comin', things weren't lookin' too good.
Nothin' was going just exactly like it should.
Everything seemed to be goin' wrong.
So I sat myself down and I wrote out this song.
I got the Science Fair blues, I got the Science Fair blues.
I don't know what I'm doin', but I'm gonna show it to you." *

---

* The whole song is in my book *All Blues*

And isn't that the way it is? We often don't know wholly what we're doing, but day after day, are thrust into the situation of presenting ourselves and doing the best we can. We take the Teaching Methods class, read the education books and nod our head in feigned understanding, but it all comes down to that moment when the school bell rings and a crowd of lively students come humming, bumping, chattering into the room. And there we are, in charge of organizing that chaotic swirl of energy. All that theory from the Methods class seems to fly out the window. We open our mouth and hope for the best, teaching with the full force of our personality, our own way of thinking and doing.

This is the order things almost always happen—the experience comes first and the concepts, ideas and theories that try to organize and explain the experience comes second. In my own case, I was thrust ill-prepared into the waters of teaching and every day splashed around trying to keep my head above water. From sheer survival instinct, I had to notice the things that worked well and the things that worked less well and give language to them. And thus was born this list of guidelines for developing material.

These guidelines can serve as a scaffolding for organizing lessons, a check-list to see where they failed or an invitation to take them into unexpected new directions. Though they were initially written for music teachers, I believe with some slight adjustment, they are sound pedagogical principles applicable to teachers in all subjects.

1. SIMPLE TO COMPLEX

> "Today we're going to learn a piece from Medieval Spain. It's part of the vast repertoire both collected and composed by Alfonso de Sabio, king of Spain between 1252 and 1284. The collection is called *Cantigas de Santa Maria*, which translates to *Songs to the Virgin Mary*. The piece we're learning is in the Dorian mode, a minor mode with a major 6th. The rhythm alternates between 6/8 and 3/4 meter, a rhythmic practice known as hemiola most commonly recognized in the song "America" from *West Side Story*. It's in an AB binary form and…. Are you all with me here?"

I think not. Most likely, we are overwhelmed and confused by the sheer volume of information coming at us so rapidly we can't digest it. Day after day, kids experience this kind of information overload at school. One of the most common mistakes beginning teachers make—and experienced ones as well—is to present **too much information at once.** " K.I.S.S.," said my mentor teacher time and time again—"Keep It Short and Simple."

I imagine we all have suffered through the experience of being taught by people whose skill we admire, but discover that they have no idea how to transmit what they know. In the music world, they might be a phenomenal player, but a terrible teacher. They are a master at what they do, but they have no idea how to make what they know understandable and accessible to a five-year-old. "Explain it to me like I'm in kindergarten," said Denzel Washington's character in the film *Philadelphia* and I quote him frequently when I'm talking to the tech support person walking me through the new app.

How to take the multiple dimensions of a particular piece of knowledge and break it down to its most basic parts? This is every teacher's challenge. Once we understand this, we discover that every student can indeed master anything if we can reduce it to its most basic (but still musical) part. Encouraged by our first success, we go from the first step to the second, building from the knowledge understood and the activity mastered. Step by step we walk with a clear endpoint in mind until lo and behold, we have arrived!

The art of teaching requires not only scientific analysis of the individual parts of a skill, concept or body of knowledge, but choosing material that is patterned in clear and understandable ways. In music, there are some beautiful melodies that have large leaps and not much repetition—like *Stardust* in the jazz world or Ralph Vaughan Williams *The Lark Ascending* in the classical world. Not good choices for your 4th grade Spring Concert! Instead, **search for supremely musical, but repetitively patterned pieces that kids can immediately grasp.**

Look at this simple Serbian dance piece called *Poskok*.

Poskok

Serbian Dance Song

The melodic structure is a short call (A) and an ascending response (B), the call repeated followed by a descending response (B¹). The new call (C) is followed by the familiar response (B) and the familiar call (A) followed by the second response (B¹). The form—ABAB/CBAB—is clear, understandable and playable.

Now comes the task of how to teach the simplest elements first. Since the two responses are consistent throughout the piece, a sequence like this is quite effective:

- Teacher plays/sings calls, students play/sing responses.
- Switch. Students do calls, teacher response.
- Half group call, half group response. Switch.
- All do all.

Throughout this process, check in with the children to see if they can describe how the piece works. You can reinforce the structure on the board with a diagram like the one above.

Once they learn the song as presented, play this variation below and ask what is different. (The passing f that connects the call and response). They're now ready to play the complete melody.

By choosing a simple, but musical, piece, analyzing the form with the students, mastering the music step-by-step, we have accomplished just about everything a music teacher could hope for:

- The students feel successful. They have tangible proof that they're musical.
- They're now motivated to master the piece yet further and open to the next piece.
- They clearly understand how the piece is constructed and have the possibility of improvising within the structure and/or composing a new piece following the form.

Understanding. Mastery. Enthusiasm. All students deserve this and are asking for it in their child-like way. So when we find ourselves with a group of discouraged students, remember that they are asking for a K.I.S.S. The kind we should give to them.

2. BODY TO INSTRUMENT

Tell someone you're a musician and what's their first question?

"What instrument do you play?"

A musician might respond:

"I'm a musician. That means I can make music on anything."

The prevailing assumption in the West is that a musician is a specialized technician who plays a particular instrument by reading notes written on paper. We associate musical intelligence with the tool rather than the person. Of course, all musicians eventually lean toward one instrument that they will put in countless hours to master and many will learn traditional notation as well. But fingers pressing keys following black-dot instructions on paper is not at the center of musicality's true nature.

Because of these notions, much music instruction formally begins when a student chooses an instrument and learns how it works. Where to put one's fingers or how to blow and how to make sounds go up or down or loud or soft. At the same time, they have to begin the long and arduous process of figuring out those dots called quarter notes, rests, middle C, and so on. That's a lot going on for the beginning student! As they say in the kids' world, TMI! *

What's the alternative? As Orff himself said:

"Music begins inside human beings and so must any instruction. Not at the instrument, not with the first finger, nor with the first position, not with the this or that chord…"

Orff suggests that teaching not begin with the instrument, but with the child. The living, breathing child who already has rhythms pulsing inside the body, who is singing as she plays, dancing when he hears music, curious about the sonic possibilities of popping leaves, blowing on grass stems, tapping water classes, drumming on tables. If we take these impulses and artfully shape them in our bodies and

---

* Too Much Information

voices, then we can draw forth and give form to all the music singing inside of us. Now when the child arrives at the instrument, she has only one thing to figure out—**how to transfer the music she can sing, move and feel onto a particular instrument.** Without that preparation, the student arrives at the instruments with ten things to master instead of one. Without first experiencing each musical element in his or her body and voice, the child pushing down keys or plucking strings has nothing to say.

And so **begin in the body.** Just about every class. Dance to the music, be it sung, played or recorded, pat the accompanying rhythms, gesture the harmonic changes, vocalize the sounds of the instruments to be used—and for goodness sake, always sing the melody! Whether that preparation takes one minute or an entire class, the children released to the instruments now have the job of playing what they can sing, figuring out how to convert those abstract tones in the air to the concrete notes on the xylophone or recorder or indeed, any instrument. Let them struggle with it a while and observe their strategies. If they make a mistake and try again, leave them alone! Don't interfere too soon and show them the "right notes." Let them exercise their aural muscles. If they peek at their neighbor, great! If they ask their friend for help, good! If they look like they're about to have a nervous breakdown, then you can casually ask, "Would you like me to help you?"

In the *Poskok* example given in the first guideline, the students learned to sing the skeleton melody. Now their job is to "find it" on the Orff instruments. If they've already analyzed the stepwise ascent and descent of the response, they will be able to easily find it on the xylophones.

The Three T's

In preparing an instrumental part, be it on percussion or melodic instruments, there are three essential qualities:

1. Timing: When does this phrase start? What is its relationship to the beat? To the meter? To the other parts?

2. Technique: How is this played on the instrument? How can we prepare the physical technique on the body before playing the instrument?
3. Tone: What kind of sound are we aiming for? What kind of timbre? Of articulation? If it's a melody, how can we sing it close to the way it sounds on the instrument?

These are useful—indeed, *essential* questions—to ask as you consider how to teach something before taking out the instrument. Take some time to think about how to best express the part you're teaching in the body and voice before moving to the instruments.

For example: In teaching a beginner how to play the hi-hat cymbal in the jazz ensemble, teach this line from a children's game: *"I said a /boom chick a rocka chick a rock a chicka boom"* * All snap on the words "chick" and "said." This way of teaching **timing** in a child-friendly is more effective and child-friendly than counting 1 2 3 4. Add a rocking motion with the left foot, with the toe going down on the snap. That teaches the **technique** of playing the hi-hat. Accent the word chick as you speak the phrase and that gives the **tone** you're aiming for in the hi-hat. Now they're ready to play the hi-hat successfully, because they've already practiced three essential things.

So when teaching percussion parts, it takes some thought as to how to map them out ahead of time on the body and in the voice. Most percussion parts are like melodic patterns with two or more tones. Not only does the relationship of the rhythm to the beat need to be made clear, but the pattern of the tones as well. Most percussionists intuitively vocalize the tonal pattern when teaching. Now is the time to make it more conscious and combine it with the physical patterns played on the body.

With melodies, the nuances of articulation are often sung or spoken to prepare the most musical expression on the particular instrument. Jazz scat "ba doo doo be doo ba!" or a kind of classical musical scat "di di di di dum dum di/ di di di di dum " prepare the

* Details of this process in my book *Now's the Time: Teaching Jazz to All Ages*

children to not only get the right notes, but hear the articulation that really makes that particular passage sing.

This simple, but potent, approach can revolutionize your music teaching and your students' music learning. Just remember the mantra of connected musicianship:

Sing what you hear. Play what you sing. Hear what you play.

3. UNISON TO ORCHESTRA

There's a joke about a bass player who arrives to play at the concert, but doesn't feel well. He decides to leave his section and sit in the audience to listen to the concert. At the end, he comes back to his fellow bassists and tells them with great excitement, "Wow! You should hear what the violins are playing!"

Playing from the written notes, he needn't actually *listen* to the other parts. Following a score can put the musicians in a tunnel of sorts where they don't necessarily hear everything happening around them. If they can play the written notes successfully and count the rests when they don't play, they don't need to know or hear how all the parts actually fit together.

Even when they do (and at the professional level they certainly do), they still are experiencing the music from one point of view only. The flute will play the melody, the guitar the chords, the bass outline the harmony, the viola play some supporting harmonies and counterpoint, the percussion some rhythmic *ostinati* or color parts. Each stays in their lane and though the result is orderly, sometimes it is as if all their windows were rolled up and they're driving along in their own private car. Especially with children in the beginning stages of ensemble playing.

So much of what we offer in schools, be it a string orchestra, a band and even a choir, is built from the notion of specialization. Knowing and hearing all the parts in a given composition is part of what sets Orff Schulwerk education apart from this way of working. * At some point in every Orff workshop, I have the teachers raise their right hand dutifully recite my Orff oath:

"I promise… that I will teach… all the parts… to all the students… all the time… so help me Orff."

This simple tenet—**teach all the parts to everyone**—is perhaps the most important and radical of all in the Orff music class. What does it mean and how does it work?

Here is *Poskok* in a classic Orff orchestration: bass xylophones playing a drone, altos an ostinato, sopranos a melody and glockenspiels a color part.

---

* Even if the band, choir or orchestra teachers were convinced of the value of all students learning all the parts, they would be faced with the obstacle of technique. "Trombones, go play the saxophones. Violins, go play the clarinet." Not likely. However, even here, tubas could play the violin part of the score and violins the tuba part and create an intriguing, if not hilarious, re-orchestration of the same piece. And of course, all could sing the other parts.

Arrange instruments in a square:

Sopranos

Glockenspiels   **Altos**

Basses

- Prepare the students with the body and voice (as noted previously) and have the first group go to the basses to play the drone while all sing the song.
- After successfully playing, they move on to the altos to play the *ostinato* while the next group comes to the basses. Both groups play and all sing.
- Continue in this way with the sopranos (melody) and glockenspiels (color).
- Keep rotating around until all have played each part at least once (some groups will have played twice).

By so doing, they get a thorough understanding of how the piece is put together, hear it from all different angles and get a chance to practice each part on the instrument.

And there is more. They also may dance the piece or sing the melody or play it on recorder or create a text or make up a dramatic interpretation of it. They are diving deep into the workings of a single piece of music and one can feel that sense of living the whole piece in the subsequent performance.

And there's a bonus: you, the teacher, don't have to plan so much! Just dig deeply into one thing from these multiple perspectives and give the kids time to sink their teeth into it all. (See chapter One Thing One Hundred Ways)

Unison to Orchestra also follows the **Simple to Complex** principle. It is much easier to play something altogether then to split it into parts. To play in unison offers the benefit of riding on the coattails of your fellow musicians, leaning on those that know the parts better, entraining with the collective pitch and rhythm, feeling the community as your teacher. To split into parts is a more sophisticated skill set, requiring the independence necessary for holding your part while other things are happening around you.

How does this principle apply to other subject areas? It's a bit like the whole class studying together a particular topic—say haiku poetry. If you began with one student studying the Japanese poet Basho, another Issa, another Buson, and never venturing beyond their chosen poet, they'd have a more narrow experience of haiku. If everyone studied all three poets and then chose one to study in more depth, it would be a richer experience for all.

Some musical ensembles are based on this kind of flexibility. Playing in a Balinese gamelan or Ghanaian drum choir, one is expected to be able to play any of the instruments and supporting parts. The ensemble leader knows all of them intimately and can teach any of them, while also holding all the parts together playing the master drum parts.

Then sports. Some, like football, are strict in their specialization. At no time does the linebacker say, "Hey, I think I'll be quarterback today!" Soccer coaches are more flexible, routinely mixing players up to try all the positions before specializing. And though basketball positions are assigned mostly on height, this sport is yet more fluid. Even the center has to dribble downcourt some time and the point guard has to grab the rebound. And they all have to play defense.

Music is unique inasmuch as, with few exceptions (mostly pianists), it is a team effort. Specialization at the highest levels is inevitable, but during the training, everyone benefits from trying out all the parts, learning how each works, even trying out most of the instruments. So next time your students have trouble keeping their part in the context of the whole music, remember your oath: "I promise to teach all the parts to all the students all the time."

4. IMITATION TO CREATION

"We are, in truth, more than half of what we are by imitation," said Lord Chesterfield and from the baby copying the mother sticking out her tongue to Martin Luther King studying the life of Gandhi, this truth is irrefutable. Before we climb on the shoulders of giants, we study the way they walk and move and feel and think and try some out for ourselves. Those photos of the father and son sitting in identical postures, the daughter watching the mother plant the garden, the neighborhood kids copying the teenagers' dance moves, are more than just cute—they capture Nature's essential strategy of initiation, the way the young ones not only try out needed skills, but also try out different identities as they grow into their own unique self.

Children enter school already educated by the power of imitation, and good teaching continues this process to great advantage. It begins with the essential physical techniques of school-learning modeled by the teacher and copied by the children—from pencil grip, scissors technique and paper folding at the beginning stages to breathing exercises, xylophone techniques and weaving techniques further up the line. Likewise, the set procedures that move knowledge forward—how to carry over in addition, diagram a sentence, transpose a musical scale—are all introduced with a given model, imitated and practiced.

But don't stop there. Once the model is mastered, ask students to "make it their own," to interpret, re-shape or extend the given material. This not only tests the depth of their comprehension, but also allows them to participate more actively, to show themselves more fully, to share their unique ideas with the class. If "more than half of what we are" comes from *imitation*, then the rest comes about through creation. We build our selves partially through each act of creation.

In our *Poskok* example, students can create a whole new melody in this hexatonic scale or elaborate the given melody keeping the skeleton intact (see example below). In either case, they're demonstrating what they understand about a variety of musical elements.

And that's when education gets interesting—for student and teacher alike. It's one thing to have a set curriculum and see the children as mere vehicles to carry the information you set before them and quite another thing to use all existing knowledge as the springboard for the child to discover his or her corner of creation. In my own music classes, I work hard at cultivating musicians who can play the works of Thelonious Monk, Bach or the Lobi xylophone tradition with confidence and competence, but much more interesting to me are the moments when the children reveal themselves to me and their classmates, surprise even themselves with the particular way they sang the song or created a new dance move or improvised on the blues.

One of the great failures of schools is stopping just before the act of creation. The modern trend of proving a school's efficacy and worth through testing lowers the whole enterprise to merely repeating what's already known. Tests can be valuable in revealing what one understands, but they are just one point on the continuum. To effectively meet the problems of today, we need to be armed with the knowledge of yesterday, but also imagine what we yet don't know about tomorrow. The right answers to yesterday's questions will only get us so far. We need the right questions for tomorrow's problems.

In short, it's not enough to know the right answer. The question to ask the children is: "Now that you know the answer, what are you going to do with it? You've learned how to craft an essay—now what do you have to say? You've mastered the exercise in perspective and answered the questions about the color wheel—now what are you going to paint? You've learned the basic information about registering all Jews in Nazi Germany—now how will you react to the new proposed laws about Latinos in Arizona?" The creative response to material is not just a fluffy artsy frill to the side of the main course of education—it is how we actively cultivate the thinkers of today and the citizens of tomorrow.

A word of warning. It is a mistake to have children merely imitate, but it also can be a problem to have them create too soon without adequate imitation. Many a creative endeavor has failed because the teacher has not sufficiently introduced the model and the children haven't spent enough time imitating and practicing is. I went to a jazz workshop once where the teacher *began* class by calling on people and shouting at them to improvise scat singing. You can imagine their dismay. Had he sung phrase after phrase and had the group echo, then asked them to vary slightly their echoed phrase, changing the rhythm or pitch, then make up a new one (question-answer instead of echo) and finally put several of their improvised phrases together to form a more extended solo improvisation, he would have had much greater success.

Each new learning must go through a period of imitation, but is completed by the invitation to create. The jazz world is a beautiful model of this process in action. Many musicians on their way up learn the solos of master musicians who have come before and imitate their styles. But the goal of the whole enterprise is to find their own voice built from the confluence of influences, their own particular way to express themselves.

Imitation to creation is more than just a good strategy of school-learning, it is the way we build a self, find out who we are and what we have to contribute.

5. AURAL TO WRITTEN

"Sound before symbol, speak before read." Can anyone doubt this obvious truth? Yet there is one field where we seem confused as to the proper order: Music.

Here is my stand-up comic version of my first piano lesson at 6 years old:

> Teacher: "Welcome to your piano lesson. Let's start by looking at this piece of paper. This is a note called C."
>
> Me: "It doesn't look like C."
>
> Teacher: "Well, true, but music notes look different from alphabet letters. Now when I point to this note, you push down this key called C."
>
> Me: "But you said that was C. Why is this C? And when I push it, it doesn't make the sound of C."
>
> Teacher: "No, it's just called C and the next one is D. Then E, F, G, A…"
>
> Me: "Wait! What happened to H? A doesn't come after G!"
>
> Teacher: "Well, in music it does. There's only 7 letters we use and then we start all over again at a new octave."
>
> Me: "Octave?"
>
> Teacher: "Never mind. Let's move on. Now if you see the C note filled in, that's called a quarter note."
>
> Me: "Quarter of what? Or are we talking about money now?"
>
> Teacher: "No, it's not that kind of quarter. There's usually 4 of them in a measure, so it's a quarter of the measure."
>
> Me: "Now we're measuring things? Do I need my ruler?"
>
> Teacher: "No, it just means a group of four beats. And a quarter note is worth one beat."
>
> Me: "Oh, I get it! So if there are three beats in a measure, is it called a third note?"

Teacher: "No and don't ask me why not! It just isn't. So now look at this piece of paper and there are four quarter note C's and when I point to them, push down this key on the piano called C four times and try to keep the beat. Ready? Go!!"

Me: "I did it! But I just have one more question."

Teacher: "I shudder to hear. What?!"

Me: "Was that music?"

And the honest answer is, "No."

Now picture this first lesson:

Teacher: "Nice to meet you. What's your name?"

Student: "Jessica."

Teacher: "Last name?"

Student: "Williams."

Teacher: "Let's clap it."

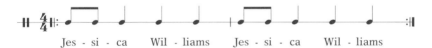

Jes - si - ca   Wil - liams   Jes - si - ca   Wil - liams

Teacher: "Favorite food?"

Student: "Sushi and sashimi."

Teacher: "Great. Pat and step it. Now the whole thing:"

Jes - si - ca   Wil - liams   su - shi and sa - shi - mi

Teacher: "Okay! See these black keys? Make up a song with your text."

Jes - si - ca   Wil - liams   su - shi and sa - shi - mi

Teacher: "How did that sound?"

Student: "Great!! We made music!!!"

Teacher: "Yes, indeed we did. Sometime later, I'll show you how you can write that song down so other people far away can learn it."

Feel the difference? Sound before symbol. Sometimes just sound stored in the voice and fingers and memory circuits of the brain without ever needing to notate it. Sometimes preserving it with audio and/or video recording instead of written symbols. Sometimes making graphic notation scores that show shapes and intensities and give space for interpretation. There are multiple ways to store and disseminate music, but all of them should *follow* the actual making of music, not precede it.

Schools, naturally, are big on literacy of all kinds—linguistic, mathematical and musical. After all, schools came into being with a simple proposition—teach children to read and write and while they're at it, 'rithmetic. The 3 R's are the foundation and it's only natural that the subjects that get the highest status are ones that can be captured in print. It's understandable that music in the schools and culture at large is associated with written notation, to the point where a musician about to play something might say, "Hold on a moment, let me get my music." And comes back with a printed score. That vibrant flowing verb of music is now reduced to pieces of paper with black dots, a concrete, tangible object that you can hold in your hands and with years and years of training, unthaw those frozen notes and get them flowing. For most of the world's musicians, that's a strange notion.

If you begin with the ear, the body, the voice, the immediate expression of music with no unnecessary intermediaries, you will be meeting young children exactly where they are. They'll be happy that they get to be themselves and happy that you understand who they are and what they need and how they think and how they play. That's the beginning. Then what?

When kids are ready for it—usually around the same time they're ready for language reading—they're fascinated to think that you can notate in print the rhyme or song they know how to play and sing. They're intrigued by how you can store and remember a rhythm or a song you invented. They're excited to think that something they write down can be read by someone else far away and made into music. They feel the power of this new knowledge.

There are various notational systems that can help lead beginning learners to traditional scores. With rhythm, the French time-name system, the Kodaly rhythmic syllables, the Gordon syllables, the newly invented Ta-Ke-Ti-Na and the millenia-old Indian Solkatu system are just some possibilities. With melody, Western solfege is commonly used. India has a similar system and some musical styles like Javanese gamelan and Chinese orchestra use a number system. Take your pick. *

How much time should be devoted to mastering notation? Few music programs, especially in the elementary years, have enough time to introduce even the most basic musicality. To be comfortably fluent readers would require music classes at least 3 or 4 times each week over many years. Because of our time restrictions, we need to pay attention to the proper order and balance between the ear and the eye.

As suggested here, aural to written is indeed the proper order. Consider how much more direct, efficient and effective the oral approach is in communicating the essential information about music. Symbolic notation has tried hard to indicate with Italian words and various icons when to play short, loud, with an accent, rubato, expressively and so on. But when music is transmitted from vibration to vibration, from voice to ear, from sound to sound, all

---

* For a look at the use of the French time-name system and solfege in an Orff Schulwerk context, see my book *Play, Sing & Dance*.

that information is present. Listen to a child imitate a pop singer and it's all there—the accent, the inflection, the style, imitated directly and immediately. To transmit that information through the written medium would take years and you could never capture the quality of Billie Holiday's voice on paper. Schools love literacy and thus insist on literate musicians, but music must enter schools on its own terms. Decide what is needed for such literacy—and rarely given in the schedule—and consider how much can be taught orally when one understands how.

As for the proper balance, keep in mind the following factors:

- The ability to hear, play and create music requires a great deal of time and experience, again, more than most music teachers in schools are allotted.
- Likewise, the ability to play music spontaneously with others in a musical conversation needs much experience in the oral world of music-making.
- Children in general music classes are there because the school decided music was a core (or at least mandatory auxiliary) subject. They have not chosen to be in music class because they're on track to become professional musicians. But they are curious about how to make organized, coherent sound with the things close at hand—their own bodies and voices and instruments with simple techniques.
- The long tedious road of mastering notation is not first on the children's list, though with a sufficient aural foundation, they indeed will be intrigued and interested at the right time and in the right amount.

In summary, the progression from aural to written, as needed, as appropriate and in the right balance, will help build a strong music program in schools. And then return to the direct aural experience of music. Get the notes off the page and into the body, the ear, the air. That's where music lives.

6. EXPERIENCE TO CONCEPT

"Give the pupils something to do, not something to learn; and the doing is of such a nature as to demand thinking; learning naturally results."

—JOHN DEWEY

In the chapter "Do It First," we discussed the utmost importance of experiencing everything in the body, first *doing* something and then discussing what we did, giving a name to it, making conscious that which was intuitive. This has been a cornerstone of all progressive education.

Amidst other qualities of progressive education is the idea that students will actually make *progress*, i.e., enlarge understanding, remember things they learned, value things they learned. Because without the foundation of doing, education remains an abstract collection of surface facts that don't wholly make sense or relate to real life experience. But as Dewey also remarked, reflecting on experience is the next vital step.

And that reflection needs language. Experience—the feel of things, the look of things, the taste of things—gives us a certain kind of understanding, but the unique human faculty of language gives us the tools to think larger. Think of babies who have seen, touched, smelled, even tasted, a flower. When they finally learn that word "flower," they now have a shorthand for identifying it, recognizing it, being able to point to it and say "flower." It begins as a noun and then come the adjectives: "big flower," "yellow flower," "pretty flower." Along come the verbs —"pick flower," "smell flower," "step on flower." The child herself is blossoming like a flower into a greater understanding, armed with the tools of language to navigate through the world.

Every school subject has its specialized vocabulary that enlarges our understanding. We advance in math by finding out what addition, subtraction, quadratic equations and geometrical progression mean, go deeper into language by learning about nouns and verbs and conjugation and alliteration. The naming of things and the naming of processes by which to manipulate things and the naming of yet larger systems of thought is the very core of education, be it formal or informal. Knowing how things work and how things fit together gives us a unique power to move more consciously through the world. We need language to help awaken that power.

Music is no exception. There is no progress without understanding both general concepts like rhythm, melody, harmony and specific concepts like appoggiatura, anacrusis, sus chords and beyond. The mistake we often make is to overwhelm the students with a flurry of nouns before they have properly experienced these qualities. By emphasizing the concept over the experience, the theory over the practice, the ability to answer questions on a test over the capacity to make something worthy with one's knowledge, we walk in backwards.

In my own case, I took a music theory class in high school and served my time with Walter Piston, but mostly it felt like math class. When I began to explore jazz on the piano, John Mehegan's theory books proved more useful as every abstract numerical chord had a living place in a jazz tune I was trying to learn. Now it all made sense in a more concrete, tangible and musical way. There isn't a jazz musician alive who hasn't worshipped at the altar of the II–V–I progression and climbed the ladder of the upper extensions of 9th, 11ths, 13ths, ascending with melodic minor or be-bop scales and such. They all know the language to describe what they do, but the goal is to marry that knowledge with the feel in their fingers, the sounds in their ears, the emotions in their heart, to make it all disappear in the heat of the improvised moment.

The Orff approach is rich with experience, but also has its lexicon of named concepts that help the student's progress. For example, in the Orff practice of elemental orchestration, the drone is a key organizing principle, providing a mostly non-changing foundation over which the other parts of the music are played. Mostly commonly played in the bass, the drone consists of one note joined with another one five steps higher—C and G, for example, which can also be described as do and sol. Since this concept will be applied repeatedly in ensemble play with the children, it's in everybody's interest that the children understand what the word "drone" means and be able to immediately apply it in their music. Some commonly used drones:

As in our "flower" example with the toddler, we begin with the noun of "drone" and then add the adjectives that define its various characters —the simple drone, broken drone, crossover drone, level drone and so on. We build a more nuanced vocabulary that leads directly to more efficient and effective music-making. Once the concept of drone is internalized, all its variations gathered under a single umbrella concept, then the work with the students takes on a new dimension. We don't need to say:

> "In this piece, you're going to play C G CC G. Okay, now on
> the next piece, you play C G high C rest. On the next piece…"

Instead, we simply can say, "Make up a drone in C pentatonic to accompany this text." If we want something more specific, we can say, "Metallophones, play a chordal level drone, xylophones, try a crossover drone." The kids now have the requisite understanding to both imitate and create what's needed, the vocabulary to map themselves in the territory of the emerging music, the tools to build a composition or explore an improvisation. Now their doing is joined with a conceptual understanding that makes everything more clear, more coherent, more *musical*. From experience to concept and back to experience now endowed with a more conscious understanding. It's a good way to teach.

Any piece embodies a multitude of key concepts and one important strategy is to decide which one to highlight in today's lesson. In the *Poskok* example, you could choose to use it as a springboard for exploring hexatonic melodies, AABB forms, call-response structures, single moving drone, improvisation through ornamentation, dance choreography and more. The key is to pick one per class and not overwhelm the students with too much information. **One thing at a time** is a useful mantra when working in this way.

Every piece of music is ripe for conceptual analysis and study, but once again, keep in mind that the point is to develop a conscious understanding of each element with the goal of playing it better or improvising or re-composing. That's what keeps it all honest.

ORDER AND CYCLES

Simple	Complex
Body	Instrument
Unison	Orchestra
Imitation	Creation
Aural	Written
Experience	Concept

Looking at the list one more time, we can clearly see that the left-hand column is a formula of sorts for Preschool teaching. Most of what we teach will be simple things through imitation and the body (or the hand using simple tools), experientially based and aurally taught to the whole group in unison with a healthy dose of play. As children progress in the elementary, middle school and beyond, they will be moving towards more complexity, using more sophisticated tools, choosing particular parts to focus on further, reading for research and writing for presentation and organization of ideas and information, creating their own compositions and choreographies combining intuition, imagination and intellect, and working hard to put it all together.

Using these guidelines as a doctor's checklist, we might discover that our lesson that didn't work so well was too complex or we asked for creation before sufficient imitation or we moved too fast to an extension of the hand before the hand knew what it was doing. Perhaps we specialized too quickly, didn't prepare the concept with sufficient experience, went too quickly to the symbol before we knew how to speak or sing or introduced the work before the children had been sufficiently motivated by the play. Or conversely, we stayed too long in the left-hand column when the children were ready and hungry to move to the right.

I have found this list extremely useful and that's the point of all these guidelines—to be a useful tool for reflection on our teaching. Where they serve to help kids feel more involved, more motivated, more themselves learning in the style that suits their age, more musical, they prove their worth. Where they don't, try something else.

THE INVERTED GUIDELINES

All ideas and philosophies run the danger of hardening into dogma—where once there were helpful guidelines, suddenly there are rigid rules. As any artist knows, some of the best art comes from knowing the rules and then breaking them—or more precisely, knowing how, when and why to break them. The above guidelines have proven helpful to me in organizing my material and in thinking about how to develop it, but in every case, I can remember classes in which the energy flowed in the other direction. Some examples:

- **Complex to Simple:** The left hemisphere of the brain learns by a linear step-by-step chain of events, while the right hemisphere sees the whole picture at once and is more naturally the child's way of learning. I once had a student who struggled learning folk dances through my sequential method, but ended up mastering some complex break-dancing by watching videos—a good reminder that sometimes it is easier for children to absorb the gestalt in one gulp then to learn it part by part. Here the teacher models the final product—a complex drum rhythm, an expressive dance step, an ornamented melody—with the students copying as they can and then breaks it down to some simpler parts as needed to clarify details.

- **Creation to Imitation:** Without any modeling from the teacher, an object—a scarf, paper plate, drum—is given to each student who freely explores it and chooses one thing to do (making circles with the scarf in the air, playing rhythms on the plate, rolling the drum on the floor). Each demonstrates what he or she has created and all imitate.

- **Instrument to Body:** Rather than transferring rhythms or melodies from the body and voice, the instrument itself suggests ways to make music. Having created something on the instrument, the students then play on their body, vocalize or sing what they played (think of Louis Armstrong and his scat-singing here). The great body percussionist Keith Terry developed his art by transferring what he played on the drums to his body.

- **Orchestra to Unison:** When students are invited to make up their own melody to a text by improvising simultaneously in the pentatonic scale, it produces an immediate orchestral effect of relatively blended sounds. Choosing one of the students' melodies that everyone learns moves it from a thick orchestral texture to a more coherent unison.

- **Written to Aural:** Graphic notation is a classic example of stimulating the imagination with a visual idea transformed into sound. Children create graphic notation scores and then play their own and others. Naturally, sight-reading traditional notation follows this progression as well.

- **Concept to Experience:** Create a piece from conceptual instructions: "Compose a piece in the mixolydian mode in 6/8 meter using a single moving drone."

So it appears that these guidelines aren't as simple as they first looked! Guidelines from which you can depart, rules than can be broken for good reason—that's the artistic way to approach these ideas.

Finally, most of them are not just linear progressions but cycles of sorts. We improvise by ear, set our piece in notation and then play it again—aural to written to aural. You start simply on jazz piano, move to great complexity and then distill your improvisations to simple, well-chosen notes over virtuosic display—simple to complex to simple.

SUMMARY

SIMPLE TO COMPLEX: Break an activity/ piece/ concept down to its simplest parts, build back up step by step to its full complexity.

BODY TO INSTRUMENT: Begin in the body and voice and then transfer all to the instrument.

UNISON TO ORCHESTRA: Teach all the parts to everyone, practice each in unison and then divide into orchestrated parts.

IMITATION TO CREATION: Begin by imitating given model, then create something new from that model.

AURAL TO WRITTEN: Learn first through the ear with direct imitation of sound and then confirm/ affirm/ preserve with notation of sound.

EXPERIENCE TO CONCEPT: First experience something, then name it and further investigate the key concept.

ACTION: Take one piece of music/ activity/ classroom lesson and move it through each of these six stages in the course of a few weeks. Note the result.

INTERLUDE II: CONNECTED MIDDLES

This section suggests ways to keep the class flowing once the initial impulse is released. Once these ideas become habitual, you will discover that you accomplish musical mastery more efficiently, more effectively, more musically.

• Keep the Engine Running

Once you get the engine of musicality running—the beat bouncing in the body, the tune singing in the ear, the xylophones ringing—keep it going! Even if you need to give a short next direction, keep those motors idling—fingers snapping while you talk, basses continuing with the drone—so all are poised to jump back in. Just as flow is one of the essential joys of a piece of music, a dependable moving stream of sound and motion uninterrupted by cell phones or unneeded explanations, so is it essential to the music class itself. Or any class.

In the midst of music, the energy in the body, our alertness, our feeling of the engine running, is a large part of what gives that satisfying feeling of flow. The frequent stops and starts typical of many musical rehearsals are disturbing to our nervous system and interrupt the pleasure of releasing ourselves to the rhythmic groove.

While there are certainly many times that we will need to stop, practice again, explain something, keep them to a minimum.

One useful strategy is to keep some part of the music going softly while you give the next direction. In the Orff Ensemble, have the bass xylophone keep playing a quiet drone. In the jazz ensemble, keep the hi-hat and ride cymbal going. In any ensemble, a rhythmic bounce or finger snap will suffice to keep the engine running. All of this keeps us fully engaged in our musical body so that music class actually feels constantly musical even as we have to tinker with and adjust the nuts and bolts of the mechanical parts.

Because very few of us are trained to teach like this, it will take some practice to get used to and require us to keep checking in with ourselves to make sure our own musical engine is up and running while we teach. I predict the results will inspire us all to keep teaching this way, as the kids mirror back the excitement, the increased musicality and the distinct pleasure of actually being in musical flow for the greater part of each class.

• Connecting Activities

It's fine to just say, "Go choose an instrument" or "Go to your table and get out your math worksheet" and much of the time, that will be the norm. But if you want your classroom to feel just a bit more interesting and memorable than the one next door, start thinking about little games and fun ways to get the kids transitioning from one activity to the next. A few examples:

- In the music class, you play a beat-passing game and those who make a mistake are out and get to choose an instrument and accompany the kids still playing the game.

- You need a strategy for choosing someone to read a passage or improvise a solo on the xylophone. Spin a pencil or mallet in the middle of the circle and see who chance has in mind.

- The kids have been sitting in a circle and now need to get to their desks. Tap or point to the kids one at a time while reciting *"Bumblebee, bumblebee, stung a man upon the knee, stung a pig upon the snout, I declare that you are out!"* Extra credit if your lesson is about animals, body parts or alliteration—you've not only connected the physical transition, but made a thematic connection as well.

• Darkroom Method *

The first time I saw a photograph develop in a darkroom, I was mesmerized by the image slowly forming on the paper, vague and undefined and then slowly coming into focus. When I set off to teach a complex body percussion pattern or xylophone piece, I often begin like this, just doing a small part with the group copying and then adding one little piece at a time. The students don't know what the final picture looks like when we start off, but little-by-little, it starts

---

* In today's digital photo world, I probably need to change the name of this strategy—some young people have no idea what I'm talking about!

to come into focus. They waver back and forth between discomfort ("Hmm. This looks tricky. I'll give it a try.") to comfort ("I got it! Oh yeah, I'm in the club!") to the next level of discomfort ("Dang! He changed it!") to comfort ("Okay, in your face! I got this one too!") to yet again discomfort ("When will he stop?!!! Enough already!!") and hopefully to a final comfort ("Okay, I think I have the whole thing. If he changes one more thing, I'm going to kill him!").

Though in fact this way of working drives some people crazy who like to know exactly where they're going at all times and how they're going to get there, this method blends surprise ("What will he do next?") with flow and models in a condensed form the way we learn everything, proceeding from the comfortable known to the slight uncomfortable (but intriguing) unknown.

Sometimes I show the whole picture first. I perform a complex dazzling body percussion pattern, for example, and then go back and build it up one phrase at a time. Like a jigsaw puzzle, the students get to see the whole image and then piece it together. This creates a different kind of surprise. People often don't believe they can learn the thing demonstrated and are astonished when they see how careful analysis of the material and building it slowly one step at a time can achieve stunning results. (see chapter on Simple to Complex).

• Theme and Variation

Theme and variation displays the human mind at its most inventive. The whole glory of the human brain is the exponential possibilities of neuron connections not available to lower life forms. Think of all the hundreds of way you can express even a simple idea. Nobody speaks from a script in everyday conversation—we are constantly varying and inventing on the spot what we're trying to say. Because so many come into music following the "script" of the written notes, they lack confidence to improvise. But what if they could learn to improvise notes as easily as they do their daily words?

I treat everything I teach the children—a song, a game, a piece of music—not only as something to be mastered, practice and enjoyed, but also as a doorway to the next possibility. "What else can we do? Let's try it fast. Slow. In opera style. In jazz style. Legato. Staccato. Try this melody in a minor scale. Play it on the xylophone. On the recorder. On the dulcimer. Can you make a new verse to this song?"

This way of working guarantees the "connected" part of "connected middle." Once the children have learned something, they keep it moving by exploring variations. This not only keeps things flowing, but it gives an extra coherence and shape and form to the class. (See Chapter 5 for more examples of this concept.)

• Rondo Form

The rondo form is the perfect balance between repetition and variation. The A section stays constant and the succeeding sections vary—A B A C A D A E A and so on. Since this works so effectively in a piece of a music or dance, why not apply it to the whole class?

For example, once you've developed a repertoire of games, you can practice and review them all in a large rondo form. In the A section, children can freely move around the room singing a game/song like *Old King Glory*. At the end of the song, the closest person will be their partner for a clapping game like *Miss Mary Mack*. At the end of that game, all leave their partner and repeat *Old King Glory*. Now they must choose a new partner and play a different clapping game like *Head and Shoulders*. Back to *Old King Glory*, then new partner and *Down by the Banks*.

King Glory is the constant A section that gets them moving around the room, the clapping games are the varied B, C, D, etc. sections. This not only gives the needed review and practice of the games in a way that flows like a larger piece of music itself, but has the advantage of mixing up the social dynamics and the kids must play each clapping game with a new partner. You can also do the reverse of the above—a constant clapping game and a variety of games/ songs to move kids through space.

• The Suite

The musical suite is an ordered sequence of pieces brought together as a whole. Each piece is often a particular dance—the allemande, courante, sarabande, minuet, gigue was a typical sequence in Bach's time, found in his English and French Suites. Though most popular in that time, there are some famous examples composed later—Tchaikovsky's *Nutcracker Suite*, Debussy's *Suite Bergamasque*, Duke Ellington's *Black, Brown and Beige Suite*.

In the music class, there can be various connecting themes that can be put together in a suite-like form. A series of dances and activities that use the contra-dance formation of two lines of partners facing each other can be the connecting thread in the class. A series of chants and rhymes that use numbers in different languages—*I 2 Buckle My Shoe, Bate Chocolate, Uno due tre, Eins Zvei Drei,*

Sasha—can connect diverse pieces within a class or be used in performance or sharing.

This way of putting things together is part of what makes each class a piece of music in which all the parts are connected and flow musically from one to another.

SUMMARY

• **KEEP THE ENGINE RUNNING: When possible, keep one part going softly while stopping to adjust another.**
• **CONNECTING ACTIVITIES: Use games, songs and dances to move kids from one place to another, from one activity to the next.**
• **DARKROOM METHOD: Teach a simplified version or fragment of the material, slowly adding the more complex steps, finally arriving at the thing itself.**
• **THEME AND VARIATION: Develop mastered material through variations.**
• **RONDO FORM: Connect pieces through repetition and variation.**
• **THE SUITE: Connect activities according to themes like physical formation or text.**

ACTION:
Plan one class in which each moment—development, transitions, practice, elaborations, is a musical moment.

CHAPTER 7—BLEND IN, STAND OUT: The Class Agreements

Everywhere I travel, I see posters on school walls reminding children to:

- TAKE CARE OF MATERIALS
- RESPECT THE TEACHER AND EACH OTHER
- WORK QUIETLY
- TRY YOUR BEST
- BE SAFE
- WORK TO SUCCEED

Lovely thoughts all. But are they working? Are our high school graduates uniformly respectful? Do they put their best foot forward in each and every endeavor? One would hope so. One would be wrong.

Would that spoken words were enough to instill character. They're a good start, but without a living culture to support and sustain them, they don't sink into the marrow. "Do as I say, not as I do" was the motto the adults in my childhood preferred and it made no sense whatsoever.

Yet words are important. They can name our intention and start us moving to the things that matter. If we are to post the school's core values on the walls, might we capture the children's attention with a more intriguing list? Something like:

- USE LOUD VOICES/ RUN INDOORS
- TAKE RISKS/ BE SAFE
- BE SERIOUS/ HAVE FUN
- LIE, CHEAT AND STEAL
- DON'T WORRY/ BE HAPPY
- BLEND IN /STAND OUT

Now the kids might be thinking, "Is the teacher really telling us we can lie, cheat and steal? Use loud voices and run indoors? And how can we stand out and blend in at the same time? Take risks and be safe? Be serious and have fun? Does he really care more us having fun than learning all the right answers for the test?" Now you have their attention.

As all teachers know, a classroom is a miniature culture held together by rules and agreements as to proper conduct. It's necessary to say them out loud and be clear about how they work. Yet as all teachers also know, simply posting them and agreeing to them doesn't automatically bring them to life. Here I suggest treating them artistically, showing how the good and bad, proper and improper, can be held in an artful way. Society chooses this over that, but art shifts the question to "*When* this and *when* that and *why* and *how* and *how much* of each?" When approached artfully, the tone shifts and kids see good behavior as an artistic discipline and naughty behavior as something that can be expressed artistically.

USE LOUD VOICES, RUN INDOORS

Adults are always complaining that kids are too loud and I'm one of them. Except when it comes time for the school plays. Suddenly everyone is saying their lines so quietly that I can't hear a thing. The same kids I sometimes ask to speak quieter and use their indoor voice now are speaking quieter and using their indoor voice—at the wrong time! So now I'm shouting:

> "Use your drama voice from the bottom of your belly! Project!
> Be bold! Own that line!"

Of course, the kids need their quiet voice for many occasions and one of the best ways to practice is through exploring opposites. Try "one two" with a gentle voice and "TIE MY SHOE!!" with a strong voice. Try it the other way: "ONE TWO!!!, then "tie my shoe." A little harder and good practice.

Teachers always tell kids not to run in the hall and I agree, but in music class they can run. But they also have to "Freeze!" when they hear the signal. Again, opposites. Run! Freeze! Walk angry! Walk happy! Music class as the place where we can do the things that the world doesn't like to see and put them in the right container. Control them so no one gets hurt. Art can be angry or sad or loud or quiet and it's the right place to express all those feelings.

TAKE RISKS/ BE SAFE

Watch people skateboarding or snowboarding or mountain climbing and you'll see people purposefully putting themselves in harm's way. We all want to be safe and comfortable, but something in us also loves to **take risks**, to put ourselves on the edge of danger, to be where things are just a bit more exciting and just scary enough to keep us awake and alert and flirting with disaster.

Skydiving, bungee jumping, biking without brakes gives us a physical thrill, but our friends and family aren't always so happy to know we're doing them. Is there another way to take risks where a missed step doesn't mean the hospital or the morgue? Something that scares us at the beginning, but then delights us when we work through our fear and try it anyway? Might singing a solo in the choir or improvising a solo in the jazz tune or showing us your motion in the middle of the dancing circle be a life-affirming risk? Keep us awake and alert and courting calamity while edging toward a surprise breakthrough?

The music class can certainly be such a place. Create classes in which each child leads an echo clap or makes up a motion. Look for the right moments to gently nudge someone into the spotlight. Give a big part in the play to the shy child.

These kinds of risks are not only important for the students, but also for you as a teacher. When the kids come into Singing Time, try improvising a blues commenting on what you see. Start off with a line with no idea ahead of time what the rhyming line will be and 16 beats to figure it out. That will keep you on your toes and have the children watching you walk the tightrope wondering if and when you'll fall. Meanwhile, you can give some useful information to certain kids who aren't with the program yet:

> "Well, we've got our hands to ourselves, facing front on the rug,
> We've got our hands to ourselves, facing front on the rug,
> But I notice somebody is not paying attention to Doug!"

Teach something you've taught before an entirely different way. Teach something you've never taught before in a familiar way. Give the kids more power than you thought they could handle. Dance expressively in front of the children to give them a model before they discover their own expressive motion. Tell a story about a time when you failed badly in something or did something you regretted. By sharing your vulnerability, you give permission to the kids to be a bit more comfortable with their own.

On the other side of the equation, people are more likely to **take risks** when they feel safe. Our job is to make sure the children all can **be safe** and their job is to help each other feel safe. That means no one makes fun of anyone or teases them, but supports them and encourages them when they take risks. This is worth saying out loud to the children in a clear, firm and stern voice:

> "You can make lots of mistakes here, you can even get a little too silly sometimes and we'll be okay. But the one thing that will never happen in this class is making someone feel unsafe by making fun of them or teasing them. Are we clear about that?"

The "No Bully" programs in schools are an important improvement over "boys will be boys"/ "mean girls" excuses. At the same time, the pecking order is as real as sibling rivalry and cannot be systematically de-programmed by following a series of steps. The deep task is to help children feel so loved and valued and welcomed and comfortable in their own skin that they don't feel the need to create an identity based on putting others down. The "rules" for a safe emotional and physical space in each classroom are important for clarity, but work best when balanced with the rewards of risk-taking in safe environments. By pairing "Be safe" with "take risks," we help walk the children down that garden path.

BE SERIOUS/ HAVE FUN

Do you notice how many of these "class agreements" work in opposites? That's where art lives, in the place where opposites both have a voice at the table. It's fun to be funny and it's seriously important to be serious. But it's best when it's the right kind of fun and the right kind of seriousness.

As a mischievous kid myself all throughout my schooling, I understand how much fun it can be to do things silly or make fun of an activity or find something funny in it. But part of me believes that this was mostly a survival strategy for things that really were boring and not worthy of my time. (Well, at least that's how I justified it. I'm sure part of it was just that I was a bad boy!)

The things I offer to the children in my music class are things that I believe are worthy of a serious effort. Meaning that they will require a certain kind of concentration and perseverance to master them and that that feeling of mastery, of accomplishment, is where such efforts pay off.

Serious doesn't mean grim faces and no humor. Webster defines it as:

1. a subject, state or activity that demands careful consideration or application.
2. acting or speaking sincerely and in earnest, rather than in a joking or half-hearted manner.

Both define well what I'm trying to get to with the kids. It is fun to make fun of things and we've built an entire culture of comedy based on that premise, from the Marx Brothers to Lucille Ball to Trevor Noah. Humor is essential to deflate self-importance, to reveal the unspoken, to hold the power-mongers accountable. If they act irresponsibly, they deserve both sincere and satirical criticism—as Stephen Colbert makes clear in the last few years of his Late Show!

But if humor is based solely on what is *not* working and is not balanced by serious efforts to create and sustain what *does*, it falls short. It then becomes an excuse not to take *anything* seriously. Note the ending of that delightful and delicious TV sitcom *Seinfeld*. Their self-involved me-first life style got them in jail when they ignored the most basic premise of being a Good Samaritan. We all have a George Costanza in us willing to knock down children while running out from a fire, but we don't want to keep feeding that personality.

When kids—or adults—try to subvert or avoid activities by doing them sloppy or silly, it's often a defense mechanism that shows that they're terribly uncomfortable with the activity and it's easier to do it wrong than to try and possibly fail. How often do some 5-year olds think they invented the idea of going in too far to the middle during the folk dance and bump into someone else? Answer—often. And they think it is so funny. And that's when I say:

> "Did anybody notice a problem in the B section of the dance?
> Yes, someone went too far and bumped into someone else.
> Now remember our "blend in" agreement? This is one of
> those times. If we all take three steps the same size in and then
> again going out, it's so beautiful because we close and open

like a flower. But one person going too far ruins the whole effect. Now I don't know whether they did it on purpose or not, because I'm sad to report, some kids think that it's fun to ruin the dance. And it *is* fun—for **them**!

But the kind of fun we have here is the kind that's fun for **everyone**. Any fool can do something sloppy, but here I want you to **have fun by doing things *well***. If you can show me that you know how to have that kind of fun, maybe we can have a Bad Dance Day where everyone does it sloppy. But first you have to know how to do it well. To be serious **and** have fun. Let's try again."

As confessed earlier, I have been known to play the trickster, prankster, make-a-joke-of role and appreciate its merits. But I've also worked on being an upstanding citizen who pays his taxes, votes responsibly and helps bring up generations of children to be their best moral, ethical and empathetic selves. My job is to bring the two aspects into conversation with each other in the classroom. I know that fun opens the channels wide to learning, motivates kids, makes things memorable and so I work hard to choose activities that are fun. They're the most fun when kids take fun seriously enough to master them. So take fun seriously and have some serious fun.

LIE, CHEAT AND STEAL

The kids in my school have changed the last verse to the kid's song *Miss Mary Mack*.

"She jumped so high, high, high, she touched the sky, sky, sky

And didn't come back, back, back, until the 4th of July-ly-ly. DON'T LIE!!!"

The message is clear. Lying is bad, bad, bad. But a certain kind of lying can be okay. For example, I often say to the kids practicing their music, "One more time. Great! Now one more time! Okay, one more time." I lie to first graders when I say "The drone is two notes. What are they?! Correct! C and G." and then reveal in 2nd grade that "actually the drone could be D and A or A and E or in fact, any two notes a fifth apart. I didn't want to tell you this in first grade because it was just too much information. But now you big second graders are ready for it! And by the way, don't tell the first graders!"

If I tell a story and add a few details that didn't actually happen to make it more interesting, that's another form of acceptable lying. Novelists do it all the time and as any good author will tell you, "Fiction is often truer than fact."

As for **cheating**, the kids should never look over at their neighbor's paper during the math test or they'll be in big trouble. But if they *don't* look over at their neighbor's xylophone while they're all trying to figure out the melody, they're in big trouble! We're all here to help each other out. That's good cheating.

Every once in a while, usually before the Spring Concert, my colleagues and I ask the children, "Okay, fess up! Who here is in the Xylophone Faker's Club? The Recorder Faker's Club? The Chorus Faker's Club? You know what we mean. You look like you're playing or moving the right fingers or singing, but you really have no idea, so you're just cheating by faking it. And hey, it's a good skill to have! But the concert is coming up and we'd rather you actually learn the notes, so let's see if we could move you out of that club in the next few days."

Finally, **stealing**. Encourage the children to listen closely to each other's improvisations, to watch each other's movements, to pay attention to each other's ideas—and then borrow the inspired ideas adding their own ideas. That's the kind of legitimate stealing artists do.

Orff teachers also! We go to workshops to gather material, but the Orff ideal is to take how one teacher does it and adapt it to your own way of thinking and your own particular group of students. You will simplify it, modify it, enlarge it, take it in a new direction as needed. Work it out with the kids offering their own ideas as well. That's how stealing in art works best.

If you lie, cheat and steal to trick others for your own selfish reasons, that is unacceptable. But if you do each for the right reasons—

to learn something better and express it deeper and generously help each other out, well, that's good in any class!

DON'T WORRY/ BE HAPPY

How would your schooling have been different if each and every teacher had said this to you?

> "Welcome to my class. I have good news for you—**no one has to be perfect in this class.** No one has to know all the right answers, no one has to get an A+ the first time on every test, no one has to try to be better than their neighbor. I do care that you will learn right answers to important questions, but I also care that you ask the right questions, many of which have more than one answer. I do want you to eventually succeed on the tests I give, but sometimes the best way is to get all the answers wrong and figure out what happened. I do want you to be the best version of yourself, but sometimes you have to be the worst version of yourself before you realize that it's no fun to make yourself and others miserable.
>
> The most important thing here is for you to try hard and when something is hard, keep going. I'll help you figure out what you might need to do better and you need to try to figure it out yourself. **Effort is everything**. As long as you're working hard, asking good questions, being helpful to each other, **you don't need to worry** if you'll succeed. I'm just looking for an inch of progress each class. I'll do my job to help that happen and you do yours, okay? Let's go!"

After such a "Welcome to my class!" talk, I imagine your stress level and anxiety would have decreased significantly. At the same time, you'd probably be inspired to indeed want to please a teacher like that and strive to be that elusive model good student.

Kids today are under increased mounting pressure to perform and it's good for exactly no one. The combination of anxious helicopter parents, increasingly competitive college (or high school or elementary or even preschool!) admissions, an unstable ever-shifting job market, all leaks down to the kids' tender psyches and has them feeling increasingly stressed, anxious and prone to panic. All of this emotional battering takes its toll on the kids, the parents, the teachers, the culture. Millions of dollars and thousands of hours of time are spent trying to remediate with therapists, learning specialists, tutors, life coaches and such what we ourselves created with the way we've organized our schools, our lives, our culture.

I say to my students:

> "Develop good work habits, read often and keep your curiosity lit, exercise your imagination, feed your capacity to be a good friend, co-worker and compassionate person and you can relax a bit about 'succeeding.' The world owes you nothing and is not impressed with your Facebook credentials, but if you live an authentic life with sincerity, my experience tells me that you can count on some kindnesses from strangers, some propitious turns of the Wheel of Fortune and the help of unseen hands who are guiding you to realize a destiny that waits you. As Mary Oliver suggests in her beautiful poem, Wild Geese:

> "You do not have to be good.

> You do not have to walk on your knees

> For a hundred miles through the desert, repenting.

> You only have to let the soft animal of your body

> Love what it loves…"

And if you follow her advice, then you just may hear the cry of the wild geese,

> "over and over announcing your place in the family of things."

Organize your classes to minimize worry, to relieve stress, to soften anxiety, to remove all unnecessary bars that kids must jump over. Let them jump over their own bars and jump joyfully!

For at the end of the matter, we are hoping to create healthy, happy children. "Come in and see our test scores!" said the banner outside one school. "Come in and see happy children at work and play!" is the unspoken motto of schools that serve as an antidote to these narrow notions of what it means to succeed. When we organize schools around the health and happiness of children, everything changes.

If we begin to believe that happiness counts, suddenly music is not off to the side of what's important in schools, but in the center. For what school subject can bring so much happiness? If we're happy, music can make us yet happier. If we're sad, it can offer comfort and give a shape and form to our sadness that helps lift us up a bit. If we're feeling disconnected with ourselves, it can help us reconnect all our scattered emotions. If we feel disconnected with others, it can help us reconnect as we play, sing and dance together.

Happy schools often have happy music programs. When you enter a school and hear the music drifting out of the music room, see kids singing to themselves as they work and play, you know you've entered a sacred space. And so I say to the kids:

> "My goal is for all of us to **leave class happier than when we walked in**. If you come in grouchy, I hope you'll go out smiling. If you come in happy, I hope you'll go out yet happier. And if things are not going well in the class—and sometimes they won't—I may just stop and ask, 'Who's happy now? Just as I thought—not so many. Let's take a breath or have a talk or change what we're doing, because there's only ten more minutes left in class to help us fulfill our goal!'

In short, *Don't Worry, Be Happy* is more than a catchy song composed by a former parent of The San Francisco School where I work. (This is true!) It's something to keep in mind as we plan and carry out our classes. And don't worry if it doesn't always work out as you planned. Just be happy. For when it does work out, the kids will be. And that's what we call success.

BLEND IN/ STAND OUT

"A chain is only as strong as its weakest link" goes the old saying and nowhere is that more true than in music. If you do a beautiful drawing and I do scribble scrabble, my sloppy picture doesn't hurt your carefully executed one. Unless I scribble-scrabble directly on your drawing. That's exactly what can happen in music because we're all drawing on the same piece of paper.

To demonstrate this, have the group sing *Twinkle Twinkle Little Star* and at the end, show with their thumbs up, down or in-between how they sounded. Each time the group sings the song, you sing out of tune or out of tempo or too loud or with different words to show how one person (you!) can make everyone else sound bad. To properly sound good, we all have to blend in so that no one stands out too much—keep the same beat, sing the same pitch, use the same words, sing at the right volume and more. If we don't, just one person doing it poorly can make 99 people doing it well sound bad.

So **blend in**. I say to the kids:

> "It's such a lovely feeling when we feel our voice blend with the others so we can't even tell which is ours and which is our neighbor's. We're just one small part of a big beautiful voice. To feel our drum part blend with the others to make such a powerful sound. To move together in the folk dance like one giant creature with many legs. When we learn to blend in like this, we feel connected to everything—our community, our neighbors, ourselves, the music, the feelings the music brings out. We can even feel connected to all the people in the past who used to sing this song, all the people in the present far away who are singing this song and all the people in the future who will sing this song. That's why blending in is one of the most wonderful gifts music offers, helping us feel a part of something wonderful that's larger than ourselves."

One of the great problems of the modern world is the sense of alienation, of feeling disconnected and alone. Whole groups might feel like an outcast from mainstream culture based on prevailing notions of normalcy according to class, religion, race or sexual identity. TV ads make us doubt ourselves as we are, promising a happier, bubbly life with the purchase of a pill, soft drink or special deodorant, only to discover that after dutifully buying it all, it fails to deliver its promise. Regardless of whether we feel privilege or are firmly in the mainstream, I imagine we all have felt that sense of being exiled from the place where we feel wholly a part of the world. We despair about the state of our bodies, feel envious of others' talent, suffer from anxiety or depression. Who amongst us has not felt at some point what Shakespeare expressed so eloquently in Sonnet 29?

> When in disgrace with fortune and men's eyes,
> I all alone be-weep my outcast state,
> And trouble deaf heaven with my bootless cries
> And look upon myself and curse my fate
> Wishing me like to one more rich in hope
> Featured like him, like him with friends possessed
> Desiring this man's art and that man's scope,
> With what I most enjoy contented least…"

We have all been there, yes? Discontent with who we are, wishing we were someone else or with someone else or living someplace else? In light of all this, wouldn't the momentary blending in with a musical group be a healing moment? Wouldn't if feel wonderful to release our solitary self to the group self? To feel part of something big and beautiful?

Our deep desire to blend in can lead us to a path of spiritual comfort. But it can be dangerous as well. Many groups invite us to blend in by demanding conformity to their norms, leaving important parts of ourselves at the door. We need to be welcomed and belong just as we are, without having to deny anything about our essential nature. The kind of welcome Mr. Rogers gave a generation of kids when he said, "I like you just the way you are."

Music just asks that you sing in tune, keep the beat and sing the right words. A note never cares to know what color skin or gender is singing. Learning to blend in in music class doesn't guarantee that we'll never feel painfully alone, but gives us at least some taste of what it feels like to join the grand chorus. It gifts us some moments of happiness and ease.

And what about **stand out**? Consider these provoking quotes:

"Today you are You, that is truer than True.

There is no one alive who is Youer than You."
—Dr. Seuss

"Be yourself. Everyone else is already taken."
—attributed to Oscar Wilde

"We are all born originals. Why is it that so many of us die copies?
—Edward Young

We're all the same in some general ways. We're also all *different* in particular ways. Think about it. Not one person out of the seven billion-plus currently living on the planet or the billions that have lived before us has our fingerprints, our face, our body, our way of feeling things and our way of thinking about the world. Not a single person out of seven billion! Even identical twins don't have the same fingerprints and each certainly has their own thoughts and feelings. So that means that the world wants us to stand out and proclaim ourselves! Here I am! I'm going to sing this song my way in my voice, make up a motion that's different, improvise a melody on the xylophone that I thought of all by myself.

By being born unique, something is set in motion that asks us to fully claim the particular person we are. And yet human society often shuts us down, asks us to be like everyone else, shows no interest in what we have to offer. It asks us to simply conform. Schools often do as well.

Encouraging young people to claim their particular genius is perhaps the most important work a teacher can do. That means offering opportunities for the children to discover precisely what that genius is and inviting them to claim it. And so I say to the kids:

"Maybe you're wondering how I can ask you to blend in and stand out at the same time?

The trick is to know when to do one or the other. In the way we learn music here, there will be plenty of opportunities to blend in and plenty of chances to stand out and take a solo. We'll play games where you go in the middle and make your own motion that we'll copy, we'll sing songs that have parts that just one person might sing alone before the group comes back in, we'll play music in which you can improvise rhythms or melodies. The person who stands out when it's time to blend in causes a lot of problems in music class, but the person who hides or tries to blend in when it's time to stand out causes another kind of problem.

If you understand this, then you'll know what I mean when I remind you, 'This is the time for blending in and I notice you're standing out. If you really need that kind of attention right now, I'll give you one minute in the center of the circle and then you need to rejoin what the whole group is doing.' Or 'I see that you're feeling a little too shy right now to lead the echo clap for the class, but I really want to know how you do that, so get ready to do it later in the class or even the next class if you need a little time.'

What's your main job here? To understand **when it's time** to blend in and **when** it's time to stand out. We need both, each at their proper time."

This kind of talk gives a whole different tone to what we call "misbehaving." Instead of simply reprimanding kids or sending them out of class or finding ourselves getting increasingly impatient and angry with them until we lash out, we now have a different frame in which to discuss what's happening. "What you're doing right now? Tell me, is it standing out or blending in? And what do we need for this activity to work? Okay, let's try it again." It doesn't solve the unsolvable constant conversation between social harmony and individual expression, but it does put it in a manageable context and noticeably improves the overall tone in the class.

Another angle: You can tell the children that you've already seen some of the worst they have to offer, but our job is to show the best parts of ourselves that no one has ever seen before. Even us! Surprise us. And surprise yourself.

It's well and good to talk to children like this, but they will need a game—or many—to bring these ideas fully alive. Enter the game *Johnny Brown*. One person goes inside a circle of singers with a scarf (the "comfort") and lays it neatly out in a square. The words describe the actions as follows:

> "Little Johnny Brown, lay your comfort down." (2x)
> Fold up the corner, Johnny Brown. (4x)
> Show us your motions, Johnny Brown. (2x)
> We can do your motion, Johnny Brown. (2x)
> Take it to your friend now, Johnny Brown. (2x) *

Here we have the quintessential game to activate the conversation between standing out and blending in. Note:

- **"Lay your comfort down"**. The "comfort" in the song is short for comforter, the quilt that keeps us warm. It also symbolizes a security blanket like Linus carries in the Peanuts cartoon. The song suggests that cradled in the circle of singers, safe and protected and seen and valued, we don't need to cling to our blanket. We are each other's comfort.
- **"Fold up the corner."** Your outward security blanket has been a good friend to you. You can thank it by folding it up neatly and tucking it away for someone else in need.
- **"Show us your motion."** Stand out and show us your uniqueness.
- **"We can do your motion."** We'll amplify and mirror back your motion to show you how beautiful you are.
- **"Take it to another."** After standing out, blend in and leave room for others.

And so the children get to bring into their bodies and hearts this perfect balance of individual self-expression and community togetherness. It makes a difference.

---

* The whole game in my book *Now's the Time* and also in *Step It Down*: Bessie Jones/ Bess Lomax Hawes

SUMMARY

USE LOUD VOICES/ RUN INDOORS: Project your lines in the play, but also whisper to draw the listener in. Run with vigor, then freeze on a dime.

TAKE RISKS/ BE SAFE: Go beyond where you think you can, make it safe for others to do the same.

BE SERIOUS/ HAVE FUN: Have fun by doing things well, accomplished by your serious effort and enthusiastic enjoyment.

LIE, CHEAT AND STEAL: Lie like a good storyteller, cheat by leaning on your neighbor, steal like an artist.

DON'T WORRY/ BE HAPPY: Relax about making mistakes, keep happiness—yours and the group's—at the forefront.

BLEND IN/ STAND OUT: Offer your small voice to the large voice to be a part of the greater music, offer your solo voice in the way only you can. Know when it's time to blend in and when to stand out.

ACTIVITY: Discuss any of the above with your students and use it to measure the success of your classes. Ask them at the end of class: "Who took a risk? Who worked seriously hard? Who had fun? Who had a moment when you felt something wonderful about blending in with the music?" Notice if the tone of your class changes when you begin talking with the children about these ways of being together rather than talking at them about how they're expected to behave.

CHAPTER 8: THE MUSICAL SCHOOL: Ceremonies and Celebrations

"And the seasons, they go round and round, and the painted ponies go up and down.

We're captive on the carousel of time…"

—Joni Mitchell

Life moves in periodical cycles and music moves in cycles and when we attend to the grand rhythms of the universe, we live more musically, more fully. We circle around and around the seasons, accepting the ups and downs with the calliope music playing. We feel the year itself as a magnificent piece of music with its enticing New Year's beginnings, its festive connected middles and its satisfying endings and bittersweet farewells. As we go "round and round and round in the circle game," there are welcome markers along the way—all the ceremonies, celebrations, rituals, festivals, that bring color and life to the long orbit around the sun.

All cultures are alive with festive celebrations. The repetition of the daily routine is balanced by the welcome variation of the holidays, a time to pause and reflect on the past, to savor the present, to look forward with resolve to an improved future. Some celebrations are designed to note seasonal cycles, some to commemorate key historical events, some to re-tell key mythological or religious stories. All create a kind of heightened experience in multiple dimensions— special foods carefully prepared and festively served, special dress or costume, special poems or stories, special music and/or dance created just for the occasion. Families, neighbors and even complete strangers are brought together and the warmth of fellow-feeling is felt more deeply. We might hug total strangers on New Year's Eve, pass forgiveness along with the turkey at the Thanksgiving family gathering, give candy to children we don't know at Halloween. Amidst the steady flow of the days, these heightened occasions stand out like peak moments in music, helping to make some moments a bit more memorable.

Music and dance are often the through-line that threads it all together. I write this from Sweden on Midsummer Day and once the decorative Maypole is hoisted upright, it is not words or numbers or scientific explanations that welcome in the summer. It is the fiddlers who start playing and the dancers who circle the Maypole. If they are to celebrate the longest day of the year and the hot weather that invites them into the lakes after the dark cold winters, then music and dance are the proper vehicles.

And so it is with so many holidays. What would Christmas be without singing together the mystery of a "silent night," the jubila-tion of "angels heard on high," the welcome warmth of "chestnuts roasting on an open fire?" Who could imagine Brazilian *Carnaval* without the pulsating rhythms of the drums and bells and the vi-brant samba dancing? And could any birthday feel complete without the "Happy Birthday" song just before blowing out the candles?

In the Western world, music is often formally presented by trained musicians to a listening audience that buys tickets to the concert. It is captured on recordings sold to consumers or played on the radio. It serves as a backdrop to our elevator rides, waiting time in the dentist office or drink with a friend in the cocktail lounge. Most of our musical experience is either active playing crafted from formal training or passive listening as musical consumers.

But in community celebrations that include music and dance, everyone joins in. When I began my career as a music educator at The San Francisco School, I was determined to give every child the foundation to become a *musician* if they so choose. I wanted to give them the foundation to become a *musical being* who is able to keep the beat, sing in tune and join in group music-making when invited. And I certainly wanted them to become an informed and sophisticated *listener*. I wanted them to feel music as the joyful community experience it can be. So it was a logical step to bring music out of its narrow role as a specialized discipline and into the wider dimension of animating school celebrations. From that vision, a ceremonial calendar slowly grew, fed from the skills cultivated in the specialized music program. Over the years, it came to help define the very character of the school.

Here's how it all began.

MUSIC AS CELEBRATION

In September of 1978, my wife Karen and I set off for a one-year trip around the world. We had both taught a few years at The San Francisco School where we would continue for some 40 years more and were hungry to sow some wild oats of adventurous travel before the settling down into family life. We drove across the country from San Francisco to New Jersey in her old Pinto, sold it to help pay for our $150 flight to London and set off with some $6000 in traveler's checks and faith that the world would provide. (It did.)

Our unspoken Mission Statement was to immerse ourselves in cultures distinct from our own, with particular attention to the music (me) and textile arts (her) of each place we visited. Our hope was to investigate the role of music and art in each culture and its presence out in the streets or fields, its place in the festival and ceremonial life.

After a couple of months in Europe, we arrived in India and found precisely the rich festival life we hoped to witness. There were double-reed snake charmers in public parks, devotional Sufi singers outside the Taj Mahal, wedding processions with bagpipes processing down the streets in Rajasthan, early morning chants to Krishna on the banks of the sacred Ganges River and extraordinary festivals in the state of Kerala where we lived for three months, complete with men waving large pom-poms standing on bejeweled elephants and accompanied by cymbals and four drums I had never seen or heard before. Two of these drums also accompanied the Kathakali Dance-drama which lasted all-night long and included singing in ancient Sanskrit, acting out stories from the Hindu epics Ramayana and Mahabaratha with exquisite hand-gestures (mudras), intricate footwork and facial expressions. These were classically trained dancer/actors and musicians, but the stories were for everyone to enjoy until the sun rose in the morning.

After five months in that remarkable country, we traveled on, taking part in Thai New Year where everyone threw water at each other, attending the elaborate shadow plays in Java, witnessing the vibrant monkey chants and masked dances in Bali. We arrived in Kyoto, Japan just in time for the Gion Masturi Festival with its procession of beautifully constructed carts with musicians sitting on top playing flutes. While there, we took part in the Bon Festival outdoor folk dances and saw some shows of Noh Theater, Kabuki Theater and Bunraku Puppet Theater, all of which seamlessly blended the arts of music, dance, drama and visual art.

What became clear to me was that I wasn't so much interested in music for music's sake, in working on my own technical mastery or being in awe of the compositional devices of great composers. What intrigued me was the way in which music created and defined and sustained community, was just one part of a greater fabric that included dance, drama, prayer, costume, masks, food, festivity, ceremony and celebration.

We returned from that rich year to our jobs at the school, a place where children would learn all that culture deemed important—the classic reading, writing and arithmetic—but with a more festive spirit, a more community approach, a more creative co-participation from the children. The school also had the wisdom to know that music and art were essential to each child's education. When

Karen was hired as the first visual arts teacher in 1974 and I was hired as the first music teacher in 1975, we each set to work creating our curriculums according to our intuitive visions. Returning from our trip in 1979, both programs were about to become much richer. The Orff approach that shaped my way of teaching was the perfect vehicle to enlarge the definition of music and teach accordingly. In Carl Orff's own words, music is:

> "…never just music alone, but is bound up with movement, dance and speech, and so it is a form of music in which one must participate, in which one is involved not as a listener, but as a co-performer."

Thus began the idea and ideal of creating a school ceremonial life bound together by music, sung, played and danced by both children and teachers and occasionally parents, made visually festive through art and often involving poetry, storytelling and drama. We sewed Balinese flags hung on bamboo poles for the children to pass under in our Opening Ceremony, created our own version of a Brazilian-inspired Samba Contest, began the Winter Solstice tradition of the old British Isles *St. George and the Dragon* play complete with the magical North Skelton Sword Dance, had the kids make large paper maché Chinese lions and dance in them for Chinese New Year. We had whimsical events like The Cookie Jar Contest, the Intery Mintery Halloween ritual,[*] the end-of-school Mud Pie Ceremony and the Hug Line (see Closing Ceremony). We created profoundly moving Martin Luther King Ceremonies, lifting our spirits as the children sang 60's protest songs. We made student-driven celebrations of Black History, Women's History, Latinx Heritage, Asian-Pacific Island Heritage that often included middle-school kids performing Spoken Word poems, singing acapella songs and dancing. Forty years later, all of these are alive and well, a vibrant part of the school calendar.

In almost all of the above, kids are playing music, singing, dancing, reciting and the teachers are as well. Much of the repertoire is

---

[*] Details can be found in my book *Intery Mintery*.

prepared in music classes, giving a yet larger purpose to the enter-prise of learning how to play music in ensembles. We also have the standard Winter Holiday plays and Spring Concerts, but the role of the children in community music-making ties it all to the greater school culture. Note that these celebrations are also opportunities for kids across grades to come together. The 6th graders play the samba rhythms for the elementary school dancers, the 3rd graders play Orff instruments with 5th graders playing recorder and 4th graders dancing in the Halloween ritual and of course, we all sing together in the large all-school ceremonies. Kids' natural pecking order and school's artificial division of grades both often emphasize division amongst the different ages. This kind of community gathering ac-cents inclusion and the sense of all ages—including the teachers and staff—celebrating together as one.

More remarkable still, we have maintained and further devel-oped and stayed loyal to these unique celebrations that gave our school its particular stamp of character for over four decades. And it is still going strong. A 50-year-old alum could come back to visit and still recognize the ceremonies and festivals he or she enjoyed all those years back.

At the same time that we honor our traditions, each celebration is always a work-in-progress, with little changes made each year that make them yet more expressive and effective and joyful. In the constant dialogue between tradition and innovation, the former has more weight. But though the changes be small and incremental, they help keep each tradition alive and vibrant and growing. Like the brain's hunger for repetition and novelty explored in Chapter 5, the children can count on the bedrock of established ways while enjoying—and sometimes contributing to—the small changes that make each forever contemporary.

ENACTING THE MISSION STATEMENT

> "A ritual is the enactment of a myth. And, by participating in
> the ritual, you are participating in the myth...."
> —Joseph Campbell

Behind the daily round of any community is an unspoken or spoken set of values that informs the way we think, act and dream. In the grand sweep of human culture, there are deep and abiding mythologies that run like underground streams shaping us, guiding us, sustaining us. They speak indirectly to us through symbols, images, stories, songs. In the contemporary world, these storied myths have been reduced to spoken Mission Statements, a short list of principles composed by committees to name the purpose of an organization and abide by it when making decisions. Just about every corporation now has some kind of Mission Statement. And so do schools.

It is good to speak out loud the unspoken ethos of a school community. It helps make values more conscious and intentional and serves as a guideline for decision-making. As noted in the chapter on class agreements, it is good to name the abiding school agreements.

And yet words have a boundary beyond which they cannot go and here is where art takes over. To dance an idea, to sing a feeling, to speak in a musical language called poetry, awakens other centers in the body-heart-mind that take in the message on a deeper level. This is what Joseph Campbell means when he states that a ritual is an enactment of a myth. The ideas and images enter the body and hit the heart. In contemporary terms, we might say that school rituals, ceremonies, celebrations are the *enactment* of the Mission Statement, driving the points home into the deeper layers of the child's psyche.

All schools have always had some semblance of this understanding. There are the small rituals of how to greet the teacher, how to take care of materials, how to be attentive when the bell rings. Some schools salute the flag as they pledge allegiance, some sing daily the National Anthem, both with respectful postures and hands across the heart. There are larger celebrations when the school hits a milestone anniversary or joins in on some holiday in the greater culture, like taking a Halloween trip to the pumpkin patch and marching around the school in costume. There are the big ceremonies of graduation, each with their own ritualistic markers sometimes involving a procession in special caps and gowns and the turning of the tassel. The idea of marking the school year with various forms of festivity is nothing new.

Many such traditions are simply passed down, often with the initial impulses lost in history. Without questioning, some traditions might speak values that feel outdated. With the rise of schools looking for different ways to educate children comes the possibility of creating new ideals come to life in new ceremonies. Private schools have often had more freedom in this regard than public ones, but today, charter schools can claim their own identity and any school theoretically has the potential to decide their own celebration calendar. For those intrigued by the idea, what are the guidelines?

- **Show, don't tell.** Reaffirm the Mission Statement by physical, artistic and imaginative ways to "speak" the verbal values.
- **Try things out.** The first invented rituals will probably feel a bit awkward, clumsy, unclear, like a first draft piece of writing. Expect that it will need some future editing and time for the kids to get used to it—say some 3 to 5 years.
- **Include the children, prepare the children**: Involving the children directly in the ceremony and preparing them by practicing key gestures, motions, spoken words, sung and played music, makes everything more meaningful for the children. It will require the same kind of attention that the formal concert does.
- **Create a sacred feeling within a secular setting**: Unless you are a private religious school, you should respect the separation of Church and State. However, the feeling tone should inspire the sense of awe and reverence and connection beyond our small selves that a church or temple or synagogue can deliver. Music well-played can draw the audience to a hushed silence and heightened attention creates a sacred moment without a single word of theology. I often say that music is religion without

dogma. It's the real deal, with no controversial names, concepts or ideas to divide. It goes right to the heart of vibrating beings resonating together. Whether your ceremony be fun, zany, frivolous or serious, aim for the feeling in the room that good ritual provides.

Below is a description of two key ceremonies at The San Francisco School that illustrate the points made above. The intention here is to provide a model from which your own school might draw inspiration. Think about what makes sense for your own school's history, population and culture and create your own way to welcome children into the school year and bid them farewell.

THE OPENING CEREMONY

We have noted that an enticing beginning is essential to good music. It sets the first sounds apart from the random noise surrounding and sets the tone (through musical tones) of all that will follow and develop. The opening themes will be worked and re-worked and brought eventually to a satisfying cadence.

We have noted that beginning each lesson with this kind of attention to an enticing beginning will make your music program yet more musical. It likewise will help make any class in any subject more coherent, connected and clear. The beginning of any enterprise is an exciting moment, that first step of an awaiting journey and it serves us well to consider how best to begin.

So with the beginning of an entire school year. Teachers may celebrate January 1st as New Year's Day or Yom Kippur, Chinese New Year, Nowruz or other cultural markings of new beginnings, but for teachers and students alike, the first day of school is the real beginning of another turn around the earth. And yet where there should be trumpets and confetti and a festive atmosphere, many schools casually greet the children and send them to their desk to start work. Or worse yet, take a state-mandated test. What kind of beginnings do the children deserve on that first day?

At The San Francisco School, the children gather in the court-yard and when the bagpipe, drum and accordion begin to play, they group around their class sign. Parents form an arch with the Balinese-style flags sewn on bamboo poles and the children begin to process under the arch into the school's Community Center. There another arch awaits them, a long line of teachers creating a tunnel with joined hands while singing a welcoming song. Class by class goes through the tunnel of singing teachers and take their place in their seats. Already the children are feeling: "This is interesting!" An enticing beginning.

Once seated, all join in an opening song, the Head of the School gives some opening remarks and the youngest elementary and oldest Middle School student come forward to ring a small Thai gong and a large Balinese gong. The youngest rings first and when the vibrations die out, the oldest rings next. They repeat this two more times and then ring together. When the sounds fade into silence, the school year has now officially begun.

Remember the principle of **sacred within secular?** There are 200 children, 50 teachers and staff, another 200 parents in the room and yet, it is pin-drop silent as all listen to the gongs. These simple vibrations create a sacred space.

Another song and then one child from each of the eight grades (preschool has its own opening day routines) lines up holding an empty glass. We speak of the responsibility we all have to pass knowledge down and acknowledge how many worthy things the 8th grader knows. A teacher fills the 8th grader's glass, who then pours it down to the 7th grader and so on down the line. Each is asked to keep a little water in the glass. We then speak of the gifts of the 1st grader—that curious, inquisitive beginner's mind open to possibility that we all should keep with us as we gain in knowledge. The first grader walks up the line with the pitcher and all pour in the remaining water in their glass, the empty glass symbolizing that sense of openness. Remember show, don't tell? Or rather, show and tell. The few well-chosen words highlight the graphic image of water as knowledge passed down and also emptied out to leave space for imagination. Again, the room of 400 plus are silent as they listen to the water pouring from glass to glass.

The eight class representatives (chosen each year by the teachers before school starts, with attention to balance in gender, race, character) then pass around an Earth Ball to symbolize care for materials and care for the earth while all sing another song.

A few more words, a few more songs and out they go singing, ready for some more opening school day activities in their classroom. A festive, welcoming, celebratory tone has been set which translates to the kids as "School is fun!!" Certain kinds of vows have been enacted and spoken out loud and off we go!

And the songs themselves?* The simple act of singing, voices joined together as one unified community, is enough. But the words of the songs are not incidental. The tunnel of teachers might be singing:

> "Welcome, welcome, everybody welcome, welcome, welcome, everybody here."

Accent on *everybody*, not just the ones that look the same, think the same, earn the same amount of money, etc.

Then comes the emphasis on working together:

> "We'll travel along, singing a song, side by side."

A reminder to enjoy the simple gifts of life:

> "Tis a gift to be simple, tis a gift to be free…"

Caring for the earth? Why not rap?

> "Well the sky is high and the ocean is deep.
> But we can't treat the planet like a garbage heap!…"

Making an intention for the year?

> "Gonna build me a mountain from a little hill… "

---

* The opening song the teachers sing changes from year to year, but some of the standards above include *Side by Side, Simple Gifts,* my own *Earth Day Rap, Gonna Build Me a Mountain* and *Siyahamba.*

The first day is the little hill. The mountain is the school year ahead.

Making an effort to work hard each school day?

> Gonna build me a daydream, from a little hope
> Gonna push that daydream up the mountain slope..."

Attending to peaceful relations? The children leave singing.

> "We are marching in the name of peace..."

The school year has begun.

CLOSING CEREMONY

From that jovial and meaningful beginning, the children set off into the day-by-day routine that helps them push their dreams and skillful development up that mountain slope one inch at a time. Most of their time will be spent getting in the groove of their daily and weekly schedule, developing the multiple themes of math, language, art, P.E., music, science like Bach keeping track of each line in a grand polyphonic composition. They will reap the benefits of that steady progress and in the hands of caring teachers passionate about their subjects, enjoy every step of the way.

They also welcome breaks from the routine, especially when they involve fun group celebrations. As they progress through the cycle of the unique ceremonies listed above, they anticipate them with delight and mark each month with these heightened moments in the school year.

And then, before we know it—wasn't it just yesterday that we sat in this room greeting the new school year?—we arrive at the last week of school. This is the time to learn the art of heartfelt farewell, to enjoy the pleasure of reflecting on achievements, to mark our move to the next step up the spiral of schooling. And as always, to make it *fun!*

And so the last week will include a Samba Contest, a staff-8th grade basketball and futsal game, class parties, slide shows depicting the year's highlights. On the last day, the 8th graders present something to the community to summarize their time at the school (some of them have been there 11 years!). This can be a speech, a poem, a work of art, a song, a dance, a music piece, a video. The important thing is that it represents who they are and speaks a bit as to how the school helped shape who they are.

Then comes the last lunch, with a special ice cream dessert called a Mud Pie and the challenge of sitting completely still for one minute looking at the Mud Pie (after having first sung the special Mud Pie song). If they move, the teacher can snatch away the Mud Pie and to earn it back, they have to sit still for *two minutes!* A little carefully orchestrated cruelty is a good addition to the ending of school and the kids love it! (And for those concerned, they rise to the challenge and shh, don't tell, but nobody actually doesn't get to eat their Mud Pie). And now it's time for the Closing Ceremony.

As we began, so do we end. Though now instead of the tunnel of singing teachers, each head teacher says a few well-chosen words about their class and gongs them up to the next grade. The kids physically get up from their seats and move up to the next row while the music teachers play one of the songs that class learned for the Spring Concert. The Head speaks a bit about the year, some of the same songs are sung—*Side by Side, Simple Gifts,* a short reprise of *Gonna Build Me a Mountain* as a way for each to take a short moment of silence to reflect on the mountain they actually climbed this year.

The youngest and oldest who rang in the school year now come up to ring it out. Again, pin-drop silence, a roaring "Summer's here!!" from the kids and out they go for the Hug Line, where they bid farewell to each of the teachers and even the 8th graders with a hug or high 5. Festive. Joyful. Meaningful. Memorable. The school year has ended.

But not quite. The next day is 8th grade Graduation, attended by parents, teachers and 7th graders. Before the ceremony officially begins, the teachers and 8th graders gather in the music room for a final circle. Earlier, some of the 11-year students had gone into every room in the school with a Tibetan bowl filled with water and rung it to absorb the vibrations of the places the kids had lived most of their lives. We pass the bowl around and each rings it while all silently reflect on their time at school, trying to remember the feeling they had on their first day and recall the highlights of their time at school. At the end, with heads bowed and hands open, the school Head sprinkles our hands with the water, we join for a final hand-squeeze and prepare to enter the Community Center. Again, a secular act with a sacred feeling.

The 7th graders begin to play the traditional *Pomp and Circumstance*, the parents rise and the teachers process in by order of tenure, followed by the graduating students. Some opening remarks and the ceremony begins. Some ten teachers have prepared a two-minute speech, each for two or three of the 32 graduates, trying to capture the essence of the student with an image or a story. Since the school strives to know and honor the unique character of each student, to uncover each one's particular talent and genius, this is the moment to publicly praise them. Some alumni have reported that the words spoken about them continued to echo on in their later life. Here are two examples of such speeches. (Keep in mind that this idea is not limited to graduation. Teachers might create a format like this at the end of the year in each class, whether or not parents or other people are present. Consider how this kind of talk might relate to your particular situation.)

> SHANE: We're under strict orders not to embarrass the students, but I may just have to break that rule. Because if you had asked me 3, 5, 7, 9 years ago, whether I could imagine giving Shane's graduation speech, I would have said, "Only if you want me to say that Shane was one of the most difficult music students I ever had." And that is the truth. From the first class at three years old all the way through elementary school, he was constantly running around doing everything but the given activity with a big smile on his face, almost always making little annoying noises and ignoring every plea to behave himself. His biggest moment in Elementary School was standing up and singing the wrong words to Frosty the Snowman.

And that makes it all the more extraordinary when I stand up and say before you that this young man moves me more than just about any student I ever had. And in 35 years of teaching, that's saying a lot. What Shane learned was not how to be a good boy and behave to please others. What he learned was how to take his random noises and turn them into music, how to take his naughty side and transform it into poetry, how to take his energy and turn it toward the band. In short, he learned how use his power in the right way. He is a testimony to the power of art to transform both ourselves and those around us. Here's what he says in his poem:

My dance can rule the world
With a little swing
It makes me happy to feel this
This thing that I use to breathe
Out my sorrows and dance
Picking up my feet: Left right Right left
I dance.

Shane was in the after-school jazz group and I found a song that I thought he could do justice to: "Dance Me to the End of Love." I didn't realize at the time what it meant for me. But Shane, we have been dancing together for 11 years and at the end of it all is a surprise that neither of us would have imagined when we first started. At the end is Love. Thank you, Shane, for teaching me to keep searching deeper and have faith in the extraordinary power lying inside every child, no matter what their behavior. And in the extraordinary power of art, no matter what the style, to help us find who we are and how we belong to this world. Keep on dancing, Shane.

JOCELYN: I don't know what I did to deserve this honor, but believe me, it is a great, great honor to get to speak about this phenomenal young woman. Maybe I earned the privilege because I recited a Langston Hughes poem at our MLK Ceremony and Jocelyn recited another one. I don't need to tell you which recitation was filled with greater style, passion and soul and which received a well-deserved standing ovation. But I'll give you a hint—it wasn't mine.

Jocelyn is a bells and whistles gal. You always know she's around, sometimes in a boisterous way, sometimes in a quiet helpful way, like the way she calmed a frightened and crying child on the plane back from Nicaragua. Her teachers called her" feisty," "sparkling," "vibrant," all with great admiration of these qualities. But it's not just that Jocelyn is filled with Spirit—she's workin' it! She's been involved in public oratory for much of her childhood and putting her soulful passion in a great container—poetry and poetic speech. And also music— playing the trumpet, soloing on the glockenspiel, dancing the Lindy Hop, Jocelyn was right there digging down into the jazz way. But it takes a poet to know a poet and I think Maya Angelou had Jocelyn in mind when she wrote:

"Now you understand Just why my head's not bowed.
I don't shout or jump about or have to talk real loud.
When you see me passing It ought to make you proud.
I say, It's in the click of my heels, the bend of my hair,
The palm of my hand, the need of my care,
'Cause I'm a woman Phenomenally.
Phenomenal woman. That's me."

That's Jocelyn.

Every time I hear of mean-spirited and hard-hearted politicians harming the world, criminals hurting others, people whose identity depends on feeling that they belong to the "right" group (race, religion, class, what have you), I wonder about their schooling. Did any teachers give a speech about them at their graduation? Did their schools bless them for the qualities of their better selves? Did they feel welcomed, known, valued and loved? If not, why not? Would they have become kinder, more compassionate, more caring people if they had felt cared for themselves? If they had been both privately and publicly respected, honored and loved, might they have learned to respect, honor and love others? I would like to think so. And meeting again or hearing about The San Francisco School alumni, this is not mere conjecture. This way of being with children day by day and this way of celebrating them in public ceremonies has made its mark. It works.

CONCLUSION

If schools are to be refreshed by a musical way of teaching, that must include a vibrant music program that informs community life and carries the music into the center of school culture. It's fine to have the usual Holiday plays and Spring Concerts and even marching bands for football games and such, but music in its larger definition can offer so much more. Imagine the excitement of a larger musical dimension, a vibrant swirl of costumed color and energy released by dancing bodies, drums, xylophones, recorders, ukuleles, violins, trumpets and more.

Most school days will be filled with the routines of good, honest work deciphering the mysteries of words, numbers, images, sounds and motions. But a calendar of practiced celebrations stiches them all together into a grand, celebratory whole. It gives a markedly different feeling tone to a school community, giving both the teachers and the children an extra pleasure in showing up each day. For many of us, school feels like—or has felt like—a chore or an endless trudge through too-brightly lit hallways or long hours to be patiently endured to claim the prize of a future diploma. Why not make school a place to welcome each season and celebrate each other, to bring color and life into each and every day with a calendar of ritual moments when the color is yet more vibrant and the life yet more exciting? And music, in the larger definition Carl Orff and others have suggested, is the connecting thread that brings it all alive, festively, memorably, deep into the muscles and bones and hidden corners of the heart.

Someone once told me there are three secrets to a life well-lived:

1. Something to look forward to.
2. Something worthy to do.
3. Someone to share it with.

A vibrant celebration calendar offers all three. Often after two days of school in September, kids are already asking about Halloween or the distant school plays. They tingle with anticipation as each event nears and get out of bed just a little bit early when the day arrives. The work we do in music class, learning all the details of putting together coherent sounds and motions, is worthy unto itself, but takes on an extra layer of meaning when it aims to bring a celebration yet more fully alive. And finally, all these celebrations are public community events, not only connecting kids across grade levels and beyond their immediate friends, but also inspiring parents to leave work to observe and partake as well.

"Teach like it's music" begins as a way to animate our music classes. It reaches further as a means to help all classes in all subjects flow more dynamically. Here it stretches yet further as a guiding principle for the whole school year, invigorating the school community with a celebration calendar that moves like a grand symphonic work. To do this more consciously, more purposefully, more musically, will help each and every school be precisely what it should be—a happy place for children, teachers and parents alike.

SUMMARY

• A LARGER DEFINITION OF MUSIC: Music is more than notes, sounds and instruments. It can include chant, poetry, song, dance, drama, ritual and more.

• ORFF SCHULWERK ATTENDS TO THIS LARGER VIEW OF MUSIC: It is the training ground for the musician who can play, sing and dance and understand music's larger role and capacity.

• THE YEAR AS MUSIC: The large rhythms and cycles of the year deserve the kind of attention that music suggests—an enticing beginning, a connected middle, a satisfying end.

• MUSIC AT THE CENTER OF CEREMONIAL LIFE: When practiced in its larger definition, music can shape and frame a ceremony and celebration, be the constant thread that drives it forward and makes it come more fully alive.

• RITUAL AS THE ENACTMENT OF COMMUNITY VALUES: Some basic principles to align celebrations with school mission: 1) Show, don't tell. 2) Try things out. 3) Include the children, prepare the children 4) Create a sacred feeling in a secular setting.

• CEREMONY AND CELEBRATION SHAPE SCHOOL CULTURE: Each school can create its own cycle of celebrations unique to its population, needs, mission and character.

_____

ACTIVITY: Review the ceremonial calendar in your school community and brainstorm ways to make it come more fully alive through music, song, dance, ritual. Consider adding new ones to mark important moments in the school year. Discuss all ideas with fellow staff members and the children themselves, taking care to align all suggestions with your school's stated values.

CHAPTER 9—LEAD LIKE IT'S MUSIC: Relationships, Systems and Musical Decision Making

The CEO of a company fell ill on a day when he had tickets to see a concert. As a gesture of kindness, he gave the tickets to the company's efficiency expert.

Next morning, the CEO was surprised to find a report from the expert on his desk:

"Dear Sir,

I was sent, by you, to the concert, the main piece of the evening being Schubert's "Unfinished Symphony," although personally I think unfinished work should be disqualified. I have watched the performance and here are some, but not all, of the malfunctions I found:

1. The most obvious problem was that they had 22 violinists play the exact same tune! Such reckless waste! I believe that at least 21 of them should be fired.

2. The drummer was doing nothing for long stretches of time. I would suggest he be put on a different clock, so we can keep an eye on him and only pay him when he actually does any work.

3. Many of the musical segments kept repeating themselves, and I fail to understand the point of having the flutes play the same segment as the oboes. If we can cut down on these repetitions, we can finish the symphony in 20 minutes instead of 2 hours.

4. Regarding the equipment: I've noticed a horrible lack of standardization when it comes to musical instruments, and especially when it comes to string instruments, I've seen small ones, big ones, one you hold under your chin and some you hold between your legs. I think that one size for all these instruments will save time, money and confusion, as well as make maintenance easier.

5. The conductor, the most senior employee, did not play as much as a single tune the entire concert, and showed a lack of respect to the customers, while standing with his back (his back!) to the audience. There were even a few times he was threatening his staff with a stick, which should never be allowed. I would suspend him with no pay until we can get to the bottom of this. Psychological counseling may be advised.

To summarize: I am quite sure that if Mr. Schubert had avoided these issues, he would have managed to finish his work, instead of leaving us with an unfinished symphony!

Kind Regards,
Barry
Efficiency Expert

This is a brilliant look at what happens when business practices are applied to art. They simply don't make sense. What works for factory production does not work for aesthetic expression. Likewise education. If we consider teaching as an artful endeavor, we should be concerned that "efficiency expert" viewpoints are indeed beginning to drive decision-making in school communities. What if we reversed the assumptions and considered how artistic practices might be applied to the business of running a school?

This book began with the premise that considering what music is and how it works can help us teach music more musically. It continued to suggest that all subjects could be taught more effectively and joyfully by considering organizing classes according to musical principles. It went on to look at how a dynamic music program can reach far beyond the music classroom to enrich all of school life through a vibrant calendar of school ceremonies and celebrations. Now it's time to consider how music can help inform the political structure of a school, how it might affect decision-making processes and procedures.

First, let's look at two models of how any society, from the family to the nation, might be organized. One is based on *relationship*, a group of people who know each other well, who nurture their shared vision and negotiate their inevitable conflicts of interest with honest communication. Some qualities of the relationship model are:

- Direct communication, live conversation between people.
- Deep listening that considers other viewpoints and enlarges perspective.
- Compromise as needed to account for diverse needs and points of view.
- Shared power, attention to equal voice.
- *Implicit* values—an unspoken ethos and understood trust.
- Flexible *agreements* open to revision are the norm.
- "We" the dominant pronoun.

This model tends to work best in intimate communities. When the collective task is felt as everyone's responsibility, the unspoken motto is "Whatever it takes to get the job done."

The other model is based on *systems* and searches for one-size-fits-all steps for problem-solving. Some qualities of the systems model include:

- A hierarchical vertical grid of decision-making.
- Power distributed unequally.
- *Explicit* values—precise rules and legal language.
- Equal treatment according to the letter of law (though the "law" may endorse unequal treatment).
- A proper practice of procedure spelled out.

- Hard and fast *rules* are the norm.
- Efficient (theoretically) decision-making.

This model tends to become necessary as communities grow to groups larger than 200 or so members. It leans towards specialization and gives specific assigned roles to groups to avoid inefficient duplication. "Do your job well and stay in your lane" is the unofficial motto.

In reality, all organizations are some kind of blend of the two. Systems can have their place in small groups and relationships in larger groups. For example, my daughter and her husband have recently instituted a weekly family meeting in their household. Since their children are seven and three years old, they don't adhere strictly to Robert's Rules of Order, read and approve minutes, make motions that must be seconded. But amidst the daily improvising all families do in this complex task of child-rearing, they are finding it helpful to have one guaranteed time a week for the family to look behind at what might have gone better and look ahead to the week to come. Little votes might be taken amidst the four of them, agreements made, deadlines set and most importantly, each has an opportunity to place themselves on the agenda and make sure their concerns are heard. And so the systematic formal procedures typical of corporate business are adapted and scaled down to the family in ways that are helpful. They increase the sense of voice, reveal the teamwork needed, guarantee a time and place for grievance and make clear who has the final say in the matters.

Meanwhile, at the other end of the spectrum, 21st century corporations are seeking to bring more of a family feeling into their meetings and decision-making processes. Group games, yoga, music-making, barbecues and such are making their way into workplaces and businesses are discovering that they're making a difference. They help foster relationships, offer a pleasure in the work place that boosts productivity and help people work better together as teams. Hierarchies are still intact—as they are in every family—but somewhat diminished as round-table discussions supplant throne-like seating arrangements. Dress is more casual, first names abound and the feeling of family in its better self is evoked.

And so here we have the two ends of the spectrum as to how institutions are run. Be they a school, business, church or other formal gathering of people, they lean toward either *Relationship* or *System* to define, create and sustain their culture. Which way they lean, how they blend the two models, makes an enormous difference.

It is in the *conversation* between the two that the best work gets done. The relationship model may decide it needs to write some things down on paper and the systems model may decide it needs to look up from the paper to the actual people discussing an issue. A healthy community is fostered when the rules of the system serve as guidelines for discussion, when the conversation is framed by some systematic procedures. It works best when system serves relationship, when all the Doodle polls and surveys and top-down decision-making matrixes are the beginning of the needed conversation between human beings, not the end.

A case in point. A school hiring a new head decides that each candidate will visit classes and be available for a question-answer period with the staff. The staff then will write down their impressions of the candidates and their preferences, which will be sent to a committee consisting of school board parents and administrators. The committee will collate the results and make the final decision.

In this systematic process, there is an attempt to include the voice of the staff, the group who will be most directly affected by the choice. The shy people who might not speak up in the staff meeting will make sure their opinions are equally heard. The individual written reflection will also ensure that each come to his or her own conclusion without being influenced by the more persuasive talkers in the group. The committee will save the staff from long hours of involvement in the hiring process and thus, make it more streamlined and efficient. So far, so good.

And yet it falls short. *After* each staff member writes a first-draft opinion, the opportunity to then discuss the candidates in a staff meeting is essential to enlarge the perspective. The enthusiasm or the doubt expressed by fellow teachers and backed up by examples of their interactions with each candidate helps shape a more complete portrait of the candidates. People's first impressions are then given a wider lens and the ensuing conversation can bring a clarity impossible to achieve when left alone with one's opinion. A straw vote might even be taken that would be passed on to the committee and all staff members would have the opportunity to amend or add to their original impressions.

If that step is missing in the attempt to streamline the process, much is lost in making a fully-informed decision. Furthermore, the committee might have its own agenda and can claim that the individual forms filled out indicated support for a certain candidate without the staff ever knowing. "Trust us" are often two suspicious words from those in power and a good system assures that such blind trust is not necessary. The secretive nature of the individual candidate evaluations without the group dialogue erodes trust. Allowing for the needed conversation after the submitted forms helps build it.

To further build a sense of shared decision-making, the committee itself might meet once more with the staff and give their impressions and first choice. If there is a disconnect between the committee's perception of what the staff wants and what the staff actually wants, then there are grounds for more discussion. Not as "efficient," but in a community-changing decision like this, efficiency is not the prime criteria. More fully informed choices born from direct conversation is.

At the end of the matter, the system may put the final decision into the hands of the committee, but at the very least, both groups will have a larger picture of the issues at hand. Here is a good example of how a flexible systematic process can leave room for the needed talks that helps people feel heard and included in key decisions.

Communities consist of living, breathing creatures and themselves are living, breathing entities constantly adjusting and shifting according to the needs of the moment. Like music!

A blend of fixed rhythms and notes that come most alive with flexible interpretations and improvisations. And that brings us directly back to the main theme of this book.

A MUSICAL PERSPECTIVE

Music is as beloved and needed as it is because it follows the contours of the human body, heart and mind. It literally changes the vital rhythms in the body—heartbeat, breath, the firings of the nervous system—to calm us down, energize us or speak out loud the rhythm already pulsating in our bodies. By creating motion in the body, it evokes e-motion. It is the language the heart understands best. Its complex threads of mathematical patterns engage the mind and sharpen the intellect. Its evocative instrumental colors awaken the imagination and set us down in worlds not physically present, but alive in our dreams.

Human health has much to do with the proper alignment of body, heart and mind and music can be a key player. If it can have that effect on each individual being, might it work equally well with the collective body, heart and mind of the human community? This is the question brought forth in this chapter. Let's begin with a musical perspective on relationship and system.

MUSICAL SYSTEMS/ MUSICAL RELATIONSHIPS

Music has its share of efficient systems, its *"set of principles or procedures according to which something is done, its organized scheme or method."* Out of the infinite number of ways sounds can be brought together, each culture, time-period, musical-style narrows the choices to some set structures. The fugue, the sonata, the 12-bar blues, the jazz standard song form, calypso, samba, heavy metal, hip-hop and a thousand or so more musical forms all testify to our need to systematize our thinking, to create rules that define musical style. These rules tend to be provisional rather than absolute, giving very specific flavors and textures to each musical genre. In some cultures, the beat defines all rhythmic relationships, in others, it is the offbeat or the clave rhythm or the 12/8 bell pattern. Time might be measured by breath rhythm, uneven metrical groupings, long cycles announced by gongs. Throughout all styles are formulaic, recognizable patterns that create a familiar vocabulary, grammar and syntax to guide the listener and player toward coherent and satisfying expression. There isn't a musician on the planet who can sidestep the long labor of thoroughly understanding the systematic thoughts and practices of any particular style. Learning and following the rules of any musical style grounds the imagination, limits the choices to awaken creativity, deepens expression through understanding of systematic concepts. For the players, composers and listeners alike, musical systems are essential.

And yet the deeper story is the unique *relationships* brought into play within each particular system, the way the composers or improvisers make the music come alive by their one-of-a-kind creation that will use the rules as needed, but artfully shape them, bend them and sometimes break them in service of the song that wants to emerge. The artful mind is flexible and attentive to the particular needs of the musical moment. No worthy composition or improvisation simply follows the rules. One might say it is the moment of slight deviation that gives the piece its character and makes it noteworthy and memorable.

As with music, so with a school community and decision-making within that community. Systems will be vital for a baseline way of working, but they cannot simply blindly obey the rules. For them to be living, breathing systems, they will need that artful flexibility and attention to the moment that the great musician embodies. And though not the only criteria for healthy decision-making, the way music works has much to offer. Let's consider how.

SYSTEMS-BASED MUSICAL ENSEMBLES

The Western symphonic orchestra is a classic example of a hierarchical social structure. Some of this has to do with prevailing European paradigms—most of this music was composed during the time of the monarchies, with its Kings and Queen, Dukes and Duchesses all the way down to the peasants. Some has to do with sheer size.

(String quartets have no conductor in front.) There is a tipping point beyond which the conversational relationship model simply is too bulky and can't work. Even in the democratic milieu of jazz, the rise of the Big Bands often necessitated a conductor in front (although the conductor was always also a player and often conducted from his or her instrument—Duke Ellington and Count Basie from the piano, Chick Webb from the drums, Louis and Dizzy with trumpet in hand.)

The Composer/ Superintendent

Might we compare the hierarchy in the Western orchestra to that in the schools? In the symphonic model, the CEO of the organization is the composer, akin to the Superintendent in our public school model. Both will make decisions that the players/teachers don't get to weigh in on. "I've written the notes. Here they are. Now play them as I've directed."

These days, Superintendents may be more politicians than educators. They may be overseeing a school system without any experience or qualifications related to education. That makes it dangerous to put them in charge of policies that can adversely affect millions of children, as well as the teachers who teach them.

Even if school Superintendents have a firm background in education, they are often beholden to other people in the hierarchy above, people who may or may not know anything worthy about good teaching. They may be lobbied and pressured by various industries that have a stake in making money off of schools—the test-making industry, computer companies, vending machine companies and the like. The betrayal of children's actual needs will be passed down to the Principals of schools, whose non-compliance might cost them their job. Even if the Superintendent and Principal have escaped the temptation to abuse their power, the teachers may not be trained to follow other's mandates or educated and invited to develop their own imaginative curriculums. In the world of schools, all of this can happen—and worse. Not only do the children suffer, but our culture and our future as well.

But the musical world has a safeguard against all of this. If the composer composes uninspired notes, the Symphony may try them out one time, but they will not survive. The conductor will not choose them for the next program, the audience will not attend. In short, the composer is accountable in the way the Superintendent is not. We have had many bad ideas pushed on schools and teachers—experimental reading programs, scripted lessons, excessive testing and the like. If we are thinking musically about these programs, then we would know when to abandon them. For just as the most musically unsophisticated audience can still recognize missed rhythms, out-of-tune notes, poorly-constructed form, so do children know immediately whether something is true and good and just right for the way they think and feel and understand the world. To find out, all we have to do is ask them.*

But unlike the musical hierarchy, the political educational hierarchy is content to keep the same bad ideas circulating, refuses to notice the audience, is reluctant to train the teachers in any kind of real way that gets their instrument singing and keeps the same horrible music circulating through the hallways like an earworm on steroids. If we attended to the musical metaphor as a new, imaginative, valid and ultimately effective way to tune up our broken system, things might change radically. The Superintendent then would then be beholden to the teachers in the same way the Composer is to the musicians and that would change everything.

The Conductor/ Principal

The school Principal and the Conductor have the same role—to make sure the teachers/players do what the superintendent/composer asks. The children and the audience alike are the recipients of these efforts and if all goes well, will leave the class/concert refreshed. In both the world of education and music, it's entirely possible that the written notes are just what the occasion calls for. The teachers/players are rigorously and thoroughly trained to get the maximum educational/expressive potential from each note, the principal/

---

* Read the children's testimonies in the Coda.

conductor ensures that conditions are ripe for success and the su-perintendent/composer has acted in good faith on behalf of truth and beauty.

In the actual world of schools, this is often far from the case. Administrators may be hired because of a business rather than a pedagogical background, akin to hiring a conductor like Efficiency Expert Barry who would run the orchestra based on the wrong principles. Formerly, schools were run by experienced teachers who knew from the inside out the fundamentals of good education. Their original title was "Principal Teacher" or "Head Master Teacher" and they functioned like the first violinists, still playing in the orchestra but with an increase in their leadership role. Even when they stopped teaching altogether, they had a pedagogical foundation on which to base future decisions and a teacher's perspective on what's needed to teach well.

Over time, these titles were shortened to "Principal" or "Head-master." By removing the word "teacher," we have forgotten the connection between the twin roles of administrator and educator. Today's administrators may know how to balance the budget and negotiate bureaucratic issues, but without a foundation of pedagogi-cal thinking, they will lack the vision necessary to good educational leadership. They become like conductors who don't know the score.

Why not hire them the same way we hire conductors?[*] Conduc-tors are higher in the hierarchy because they are expected to know all the parts of the music and be firmly in touch with each section of the orchestra. If they ignore the woodwinds and show favoritism to the strings, the music will suffer. The triangle player and the first violinists have different roles and different weight in the overall music, but each is ultimately essential and the conductor must relate effectively to each.

A Principal trained like a conductor will know the depths of education in its many facets, understand how to bring out each in turn and help shape them toward mastery and be aware of the flow

---

[*] The Berlin Philharmonic actually grants the power to hire and fire conductors to the musicians in the orchestra. That's a model schools might consider!

of the myriad parts each and every day. When the music flounders, they are accountable to help it sing more truly and take responsibility when they themselves missed the cue.

The Musician/ Teacher

On the lower end of the hierarchy sit the musicians and the teachers. In terms of status and pay and working hours, they are clearly below the upper echelons. And yet, without them, there would be no music, there would be no education.

Their responsibility is to know their instrument, put in the hours to practice and master it, to know their musical part and understand how it contributes to the whole. They are beholden to the audience who listens/ the children they teach. They are responsible for bringing beauty, intelligence and mastery into the room, whether it be through the vehicle of music or education.

And thus, accountable if they fall short, first and foremost by the audience/ children who will immediately notice when things are out-of-tune. The Conductor/ Principal may call them to task, but only for the right reasons—they're not doing their job well. "Well" by the standards just mentioned, alongside the expectations of preparing their part, showing up on time, collaborating with their fellow players. If they insult the audience or show up with a bad attitude, these are grounds for critique. However, if they refuse to play bad music handed down to them or politely insist on supportive conditions for genuine mastery or ask to be included in the conversation as to how it could be better, these are not the proper grounds for rebuke from above.

I personally am painfully aware that some teachers fall short, damage the public's view of teachers, hurt the children intellectually, emotionally and sometimes even physically and their accountability in these matters is not up for debate. However, in the school where I have taught for a lifetime, 100% of the teachers work far beyond their job description, are passionate about their field, love to teach and love the children they teach. On weekends and summers, I train teachers who give up Saturdays and a few summer weeks at the beach to further their professional development. I also hear the horror stories of teachers at the low end of the power structure (i.e., all of us!) whose passion for teaching is shut down by unthinking rule-makers from above that neither know children in general nor know the children we teach.

On the other side, I also personally know some inspired administrators who work long, thankless hours trying to keep the music playing and often have to deal with the teachers falling short of the mark. Like conductors working with an inferior orchestra, there is great frustration in building the school community as one would hope it would be.

When this systematic model works well, each level of the hierarchy is seen as necessary to the grand venture of art and education and artful education. The composer, conductor, musicians and audience, the superintendent, principal, teachers and students, are four sides of a unified enterprise. To be a good team-player means taking responsibility for one's role and being accountable to it. When we treat the enterprise like a musical endeavor, each striving to play their part with integrity and enthusiasm, everyone is refreshed. It works.

But the systematic symphonic model is not the only possibility. There's more.

JAZZ DEMOCRATIC MODEL

While Americans still enjoy the European symphonic inheritance—and rightly so—we also have our own homegrown music that relates more directly to who we are as a nation—or at least who we might become. As Wynton Marsalis once said:

> "Jazz is what America could become if it ever became itself."

The history of jazz tells just about everything we need to know about who we have been, who we are and who we might be. Its story truthfully told is the good, bad and the ugly about the creation and perpetuation of brutal and inhuman systems, broken promises, unearned privileges tenaciously defended, purposeful ignorance manufactured by those in power and through it all, extraordinary triumph and beauty. This is not the place to tell that story, but it is precisely the place to highlight the very different kind of ensemble jazz music helped create that has everything to do with inclusion, voice, good listening and great democracy at work. In both size and scope, jazz offers a markedly different model than the European Symphonic one.

In the small jazz combo, there might be a leader based on musical vision and a headliner's name, but that leader functions quite differently from the symphonic composer or conductor. Some notable differences:

- The leader may be the composer, but is also the player in the ensemble, conducting from within.
- Any band member might also be the composer. Or the band may play other composers' work.
- No matter who is the composer, the expectation is that the band has the freedom and challenge to make it uniquely their own.
- The band leader is like the principal, organizing the rehearsals, the tour, the finances and often in charge of the set list. But again, she or he is also a player in the group, akin to the aforementioned Principal Teacher, in the field while also leading.
- The bandmembers can not only also be the composers and contribute to details like the set list, but are given the autonomy to play exactly what they hear in each piece and often solo as well.
- Instead of *rules*, the music offers *flexible guidelines* within which the players improvise individually and collectively.
- The most important skills are the abilities to *listen* and *respond*.

How might this relate to teachers working together in schools?

Peanut Table Discussions

Back in the mid-70's when I first began working at my school, there were 5 classroom teachers in the elementary school, one administrator (the former 2nd grade teacher) and 2 specialists—the art teacher (my wife) and the music teacher (me). Every week at staff meeting, the eight of us sat around a parent-made low table shaped like a peanut to discuss what needed discussion. Naturally, the nuts and bolts of things like who would bring the next staff snack and who could trade Thursday's carpool, but also talking about kids and also growing vision. Might we eventually hire a P.E. teacher? (We did). A Spanish teacher? (We did.) A part-time drama teacher? (We did.) Shall we go camping for five days instead of six? (Yes, we shall). And so on.

Those peanut-table discussions were like a fabulous jazz band, each contributing their point of view, each listening to the others. We ourselves creating the set list (agenda) and were responsible for our decisions. We kept whatever would beautify the experience of the children in the foreground of decision-making. When we discussed things, we let the tune stretch out and weren't beholden to 3-minute recording restrictions. We paid attention to contrast, creating a schedule that allowed for different keys, different tempos, different feelings in the set list of the week. Of course, there were missed notes and dropped beats and times when things weren't swinging, but we always trusted our ear to notice them and adjust accordingly.

This model of meeting offered the following features:

1. We rotated who would run the meeting.
2. We made time to thoroughly discuss any issue, to consider it from many angles before arriving at any decisions.
3. We went with majority vote, but aimed for consensus in decision-making.
4. We made change based on our perceived needs of the children, our enthusiasm for any proposal, and our commitment to checking in and adjusting as needed once new ideas were set in motion.
5. We included parent voice and student voice as age-appropriate, but the people truly in charge were ourselves, the teachers.

Inclusive voice. Thorough discussion. Shared vision. From these simple processes, we built a school brick by brick. And like the Roman architects who were required by law to stand under the arches they designed when the scaffolding was taken away, we lived with the consequences of our decisions and fully owned them. And it worked.

All of the above both depended on and helped cultivate a *relationship* model of running an institution. Back in those days, there was no entity called "Admin." There was no "us and them"—we were always a "we."

With the growth of the school size and the change in the times, much has been lost. Agendas are pre-set and timed and always run by an administrator, "we" has sometimes prevailed, but often shifted to "us" (teachers) and "them" (administrators), there is a marked power imbalance and the music that used to swing like a hot jazz band is now sometimes like pre-programmed music or disco or voice limited to Karaoke (you can sing the songs only on our list).

Yet in the midst of all these changes, it is possible for the spirit of the Peanut Table to live on. In spite of different times, increasing legal constraints, growing parent entitlement, the invasion of old corporate models, the epidemic of machines handling communications through systems with company names and more symptoms of the "us" and "them" mentality, the feeling of small group jazz can still ring in the halls. All we need is to name the vision that feeds the way human beings actually like to gather together, that keeps the children's souls in mind, that offers teachers the trust, support and encouragement they deserve—and then get to work to negotiate our own particular blend of system and relationship to make it all come alive.

MUSICAL DECISION-MAKING

"With this faith, we will be able to transform the jangling discords of our nation into a beautiful symphony of brotherhood."

—Martin Luther King

Musical metaphors alone can't solve conflict. But they can give a useful frame of reference as to how to think about conflict. Dr. King suggests above that the institutionally approved-racism that brought out the worst in us was like untrained musicians who never practiced just banging on a piano. If we could only understand how consciously composed music could soothe the souls of oppressor and victim alike, work more seriously and more intentionally to resolve the discords, then we all could bask in the soothing glory of a grand symphony born from our efforts. Like musicians, we need clear intention, a disciplined daily practice and a good ear for harmonious beauty over jangled noise.

Here "Teach like it's music" stretches further to "Lead like it's music." "An artful approach to education" elongates to "an artful approach to educational decision-making." Since art has proven to refresh our spirits, enlarge our souls, join us together, why not bring its way of harmonizing opposing lines into each and every aspect of schools?

Let's look now at the details of how music might enter the conversation of school policy-making.

Transposition in music means taking a melody and its harmonies written in one key and moving it to another key. The relationships within the music stay the same, but by playing it higher or lower, the body reacts and the music is given a new perspective. How can we transpose music's effect on our individual body/heart/mind to the community body/heart/mind? The various key issues any school must face—class length, schedule, conflicting opinions, proposed changes—can all be enlivened and made clearer by considering musical criteria to decision-making. By looking at these issues from a musical perspective, we can enlarge the conversation and aim for healthy outcomes based on what we know about how music works. Use your imagination and consider the following:

Groove and class length: We are rhythmic beings and rhythm not only brings pleasure in music, but also drives our experience of time in all things. One of the key components that makes things flow, that brings an efficiency to our work and helps us feel "in the zone" is called *groove*.

In many musical styles, a rhythmic groove drives the music forward, enters the body of the listener-player to get the head-nodding, the toe-tapping, the hips-swaying. Once in the *groove*, time and effort take on another dimension. The groove creates a kind of tail wind that makes physical effort more relaxed and efficient and gives it an extra push that brings pleasure as well. This is why traditionally, rhythmic work like pounding grain, hauling up anchors, hammering railroad spikes, have often been accompanied by song. It not only unifies a group rhythm, but brings life to an otherwise repetitive and boring task.

Groove needs a certain amount of time for the body to align itself with its life-giving repetitions. Studies have shown that it takes about 20 minutes for our minds and bodies to get into a groove of a task and begin to enjoy its benefits. In one study, it was noted that doctors on call who bought hot tubs rarely used them. Sub-consciously, their bodies knew that it would be too much of a shock to the system to have to get out just as they were beginning to acclimate.

Now look at class length. The 30-minute class may find kids unconsciously resisting engagement knowing that just as they were settling into the groove, they would have to leave. This helps explain why a 45-minute class time is a better choice. The first 20 minutes establish the groove and flow, the next 25 reap the benefit.

The adult body carries different rhythmic cycles than the child's. Most music education conferences and courses are scheduled in 90 minute blocks. How did this come to be? There seems to be some intuitive understanding about the 45-minute cycle for kids and

90-minute cycle for adults. Naturally, we acclimate to different timings, but I can testify that when teaching in conferences that have randomly decided on 75-minute sessions, I find that the class feels rushed and lacking in the full rhythm of build-up, the work itself and concluding steps.

School meetings also tend toward the 90-minute time slot and as we consider them in the schedule, we would do well to attend to that sense of groove that 90 minutes offers. It allows us to structure the meeting according to the same enticing beginnings, connected middles and satisfying endings that work so well in the classroom.

Musical form and schedule: Form is to music as schedule is to teaching. Musical form is a type of macro-rhythm, dividing a piece into larger segments of time that repeat and vary. Just as the smaller units of rhythm—beats, ostinato, meter and such—bring a pleasure to us, so do the larger rhythmic cycles of melodic phrases and musical sections. Viewing our daily schedule from a musical perspective, we see that the happiness of our day depends somewhat on a sense of rhythm in its different phases. We enjoy a sense of unfolding with the form of the day with its morning, afternoon and evening qualities, each a distinct section within the day's music.

When it comes to teaching, schedule is all. If you want to see a group of teachers go ballistic, tell them that their schedule has been changed. It would be like commanding Beethoven to begin the 5th Symphony with his second movement or worse yet, begin on Bar 5. No matter how inspired our teaching or dynamic our individual classes, we will need a workable daily and weekly schedule to support us. What are the key components of a good schedule?

• **Number of classes:** Though there is no magic formula, a friendly morning schedule might include two 45-minute classes, a fifteen-thirty minute break and two more classes until lunch. Two more classes in the afternoon is enough. Six total—like a Bach Suite!

• **Breaks:** We need them. In teaching, music and life. All music requires some space and silence, from the rest between musical phrases to the pause between musical movements or one song and the next in the concert, to a 15 to 30 minute break in the jazz set before coming back for part two. Likewise, our daily schedule.

If needed, one could ride with the fresh morning energy and begin the day with three back-to-back classes. Lunch should be between 30 and 45 minutes and if you're in Europe, 90 minutes to 2 hours, a much more civilized approach. Two more classes after lunch is enough. Then a once-a-week afternoon meeting with your fellow teachers, occasional after-school clubs or projects, time to clean or prepare the classroom.

• **Variety:** Some large schools have music teachers teaching up to eight sections of one grade. The same lesson eight times. What you gain in clarity as to how to teach that lesson, you lose in energy and enthusiasm. Better to follow the "criss-cross-applesauce" model of "three times is enough." The first with great enthusiasm (Romance), the second working out the kinks (Precision), the third enjoying the clarity achieved while keeping the enthusiasm (Synthesis).

Variety across ages is another way to keep us on our toes. Teaching a class of 8th graders followed by the 3-years old not only will make our day interesting, but feeds our mastery of our craft. A bit like composers choosing a variety of genres—a sonata, a chorale, a string quartet—rather than composing solely within one style.

• **Weekly Rotation**

In my school, I see each group twice a week and I prefer to have them two days apart. This gives the students enough time to digest the musical meal and then return to the next course while it's still relatively fresh. If classes fall on Monday and Friday, there's too much time between the two. If it's two days in a row, it's okay but not ideal with five more days before the next class.

Again, the principle is that a musical theme is stated and then something else happens before returning to that theme. So music one day, art the next, back to music, back to art. A B A B.

One of many possible musical forms, but the important thing is to think in this way about the overall rhythm of the teacher's and the student's week. It makes a difference.

Many schools are using six or seven- day rotation schedules. We adaptable music teachers can do it, but it is profoundly anti-musical. We thrive on predictable repetition. We want to be sure that the musical theme will always return on bar 9 and don't like the sense of knowing it could be bar 9 one week and bar 7 the next. Each day with its own character set by the musical theme of the day's schedule is a healthy way for students to feel some solid ground beneath their feet in a chaotic world and an equally healthy way for the teachers to prepare their classes according to a dependable schedule.

• Special Events

Once the schedule is firmly established and has found its rhythm, a break from that rhythm gives a welcome surprise. As expressed in the chapter on repetition and variation, our brains and our lives are built on the equal pleasures of predictable repetition and surprising variation. Once the schedule is flowing, we are most likely to remember the surprising changes—the unexpected field trip, the early dismissal for extra recess, the teacher deciding on a hot day to abandon the plan and go up to the corner store for popsicles. And then predictable changes as well—play rehearsals, science fair preparations, literary teas and celebrations as noted in Chapter 8. Like the jazz player following the chords of the tune's schedule and then playing the notes outside of the predictable scale, the needed routine schedule is animated by these refreshing variations.

Many grew up thinking that rhythm meant counting beats, but rhythm is literally the heartbeat of life—in the body with its heartbeat and breath-rhythm, its walking rhythm, its cycles of hunger and satiation, sleep and awakening. And outside the body as well, with recurring cycles of time, the sunrises and sunsets, the tides, the ebb and flow of living creatures synchronized in some grand rhythmic drum circle. So why not organize our working schedules around the rhythms of body cycles, the rhythms of the brain and the breath and the nervous system? Trust your body's intelligence as to which schedule aligns with its cycles, your mind's sense of how much repetition is needed to feel the groove and flow. In contrast to our corporate Efficiency Expert's ideas, good rhythm is the ultimate efficiency. Let's pay attention to it.

Harmony and School Mission: A mission statement is like a set chord progression that determines which melody notes will easily flow within its structure. If a school makes a B-scale decision over the C-chord Mission Statement, the community will feel out-of-tune. Generally, dissonance produces a sense of unease in the body, be it the physical body of the listener or the social body of the community whose actions and words are not properly aligned. It's easy enough to name the notes of the C scale that go with the C chord, but not easy to know when to play them and which of the scale notes don't always fit the chord well. Likewise, no Mission Statement speaks of making kids suffer from needless tests or making teachers feel dispirited because of ignorant top-down decisions, but many schools have trouble actually playing the right notes to make their Mission Statement really sing. How can music and musical metaphors help create a sense of harmony in schools?

Dictionaries define harmony first and foremost as a pleasing combination of sounds in a chord, but also note that it can refer to any pleasing arrangement of parts—thoughts, words, feelings, shapes. It also often describes agreement, accord, internal tranquility and peace. Since the same word is used for sounds and social relations, we might learn something from the way sounds come together.

• **Consonance and Dissonance**
Much music is based on the interplay between consonance and dissonance. Though dissonance is subjective, even very young children already have a sense of what sounds right and pleasing and what sounds harsh, clashing, discordant, unresolved. Some of this is cultural. In Bulgaria, two people sometimes sing a 2nd apart, an interval normally felt by Western Europeans as dissonant. Yet

Bulgarian children hearing this since birth will naturally feel it as normal—if not consonant, at least a delicious dissonance.

There is an objective physics to consonance, a natural law known as the overtone series. Simply explained, sound is vibration and each pitched sound, be it a string or column of air, vibrates at its full length to produce a fundamental tone. But it also vibrates at half its length to produce a softer overtone that blends with the fundamental. And then at ⅓ its length, ¼ its length and so on in different ratios that produce yet higher tones. The space between the tones, known as intervals, also gets shorter and shorter, from the octave to the fifth to the fourth to the third and so on. Below is a simple diagram:

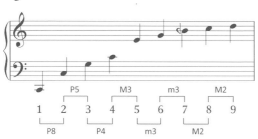

This explains why two tones sounded together at the octave or fifth or third blend pleasingly in our hearing. Note also that the first six notes together (here in the key of C, but can be in any key) produce the major triad that has formed the cornerstone of consonance in Western composed music.

But wouldn't music be boring if we only used the notes in the C triad? We need all the other notes in the C scale to create a tension that makes things interesting. And just how those temporary dissonances aim for a consonant resolution is the very stuff of artful music making. And art in any discipline. Who would want to read a story where a happy family goes through each day smiling and treating each other lovingly every minute of the day? The whole story must have conflict and tension to move it along, to make it interesting, to make it *real*. "My parents wanted me to be a doctor, but I dreamed day and night of becoming a music teacher" opens the novel and now we're interested enough to turn the page.

And so all music, stories, art—well, life—is the conversation between consonance and dissonance. We need tension to move things forward, to make us long for release. We need dissonance to lead us to consonance so we can feel both the pain of exile and the pleasure of homecoming. It is the constant interplay of conflict and accord that makes life both difficult and interesting. Music is one way to remind us that this is both necessary and beautiful. There is no question that with any community of human beings, there will be conflict and discord. The question is how an organization deals with it. Music offers some helpful images and suggestions.

Useful Ideas about Consonance and Dissonance

• **Any dissonance is usually a half-step away from consonance.**
When conflict arises, stop endlessly repeating the clashing note and look for the right note to resolve it.

• **Dissonance is a consonance not yet fully understood.**
It is the job of the listener to grow larger ears and learn to accept and even enjoy sounds—and rhythms—initially perceived as harsh or chaotic. That is also the job of
the music educator, to reveal the order within the apparent chaos.

One of my finest moments as a music teacher came in a jazz course I was teaching for adults. I played a recording of Charlie Parker improvising on a tune in which he never plays the melody. I then revealed the hidden melody—Gershwin's *Embraceable You*—and had the group sing it along with the recording. One of the student's eyes went wide with wonder and he breathlessly exclaimed,

> "Wow! The first time we listened, it sounded like a discordant jumble of random notes. I couldn't follow it and wondered why all these people thought Charlie Parker was a genius. But when we sang along, every note made perfect sense and even sounded tame and soothing! That was amazing!!"

If we have the right key to open our understanding, chaos becomes order, dissonance becomes consonance, confusion becomes clarity. In life also.

• **Yesterday's dissonance is today's consonance.** In music, there are combinations of scales and chords that Wagner used that would have been intolerable in Bach's time, tones that Thelonious Monk and Dizzy Gillespie played without resolution that Louis Armstrong would have been compelled to resolve. (In my own lifetime, the shifting attitudes about cigarette smoking, gay marriage, inter-racial marriage, marijuana, women's rights are becoming commonplace values that were unthinkable a mere 60 years ago). Another way to think about this is to compare the Overtone Series to the Hindu Chakras or Jacob's ladder or Evolution's timeline. As you ascend, you are capable of seeing more, holding more conflicting viewpoints, accepting more that you previously felt was intolerable as not only tolerable, but pleasing.

• **Two voices together can create a third voice more interesting than either alone.** In speaking, it is intolerable for two people to speak at the same time. But in music, two lines—or three, four, five and even more—can speak simultaneously to create a larger sound that needs the contrast in voices to be interesting. Agreement doesn't mean everyone singing the same notes in the same rhythm at the same time all the time. When composing, parallel rhythms and melodies get the teacher's red pen. It is **complementary rhythms** and **contrary melodic motion** that gets the music really singing, two things tastefully put into **some kind of accord to create a third thing larger than either of them.** Thus, **initial disagreement is an opportunity** to find a way for each line to keep its integrity while enhancing rather than shutting down the other line. Politicians, take note!

In all of the above, systematic thinking is driven by attention to relationship, all compositional rules are provisional and flexible and true only within the framework of how much apparent dissonance we can comfortably hold. It's always a work in progress.

Changes and Change

In jazz, the harmonic structure of a song is called the changes. These are the chords that make the melody sing out. When you find the right chords to accompany the melody, you stick with them.

But not dogmatically or rigidly, following the exact rhythms and notes as written by the composer. Your challenge—and pleasure—as a jazz musician is to constantly re-compose the song according to your own way of hearing and speaking and understanding.

You can keep the harmonic changes stable and concentrate on small changes in the melody—the phrasing, the inflection, the accent, the rhythm, the tone. You can keep the melody stable and recompose the harmony through shifts in the chord progression, new voicings, upper chord extensions. And when the soloists improvise by changing, elaborating on and decorating the melody, they always keep the harmonic changes in mind. They may use some notes outside of the scale to increase the tension, but it's always with the changes in mind.

All of this keeps the music fresh, vibrant and flowing. It is based on the truth that change is both inevitable and desirable and our job is to learn how to flow with it, align ourselves with the changes. In that spirit, jazz musicians may still play a song almost 100 years old like *Bye Bye Blackbird*, but in a significantly different style from the original recording marked by all the changes in the jazz aesthetic since that time.

But note that all the changes above are small and incremental, respectful of and attentive to the original composition. Each suggested change must prove itself by its relation to the original changes, its integrity in seeking to make the piece yet more interesting and beautiful, its disciplined and hard-won effort to do the necessary work to craft a coherent and needed statement.

To transpose this to top-down changes proposed in schools, the right questions are:

• How does this new proposed melody fit the chords of the school vision?

- How do the new proposed chords help the melody of our teaching sing out more?
- Did this proposal grow organically out of our old songs with the intention to make them more interesting and beautiful?
- Who has done the work to coherently recompose it and how are they qualified to do that?
- If the old song has grown flat, how might we collectively revive it?

Looking at how music works and considering what it can offer social institutions offers a fresh viewpoint to a serious issue. With so many "latest and greatest" ideas out there at education conferences, a shifting political climate and a dizzying array of new technological devices, schools have been more vulnerable than ever before to adopting the "method du jour" without sufficient forethoughts as to why and how and how much. There is no true north in the pedagogical compass that helps school boards, administrators or teachers know if an idea or proposed practice is truly worthy, needed and effective. Why not consider the age-old tried-and-true principles of good music and see how they might relate to good choices about education?

SUMMARY

- **COMMUNITIES OFTEN ARE ORGANIZED BY RELATIONSHIPS OR SYSTEMS:** The way decisions are made, conflicts negotiated and vision is shaped will depend on which is the dominant mode.

- **RELATIONSHIPS REQUIRE SMALL GROUPS OR SUB-GROUPS WITHIN LARGER GROUPS:** The emphasis on shared agreements, an implicit ethos, direct conversation requires enough intimacy for people to know each other and time to talk.

- **SYSTEMS ARE NEEDED FOR LARGER GROUPS:** The emphasis on clear systematic procedures, an explicit legal structure, a hierarchy of decision-making comes into play when communities grow larger.

- **RELATIONSHIPS AND SYSTEMS ARE NOT MUTUALLY EXCLUSIVE:** Most institutions are run by a combination of the two models. Those in which the systems support the relationships tend to create a sense of investment, trust, motivation and inclusion.

- **THE SYSTEMATIC STRUCTURE OF THE WESTERN SYMPHONY CAN INFORM HOW SCHOOLS ARE ORGANIZED:** The interplay between composer, conductor, musician, audience, each with their own specific role to play in service of the music can offer a model to the superintendent, principal, teacher and student relationships in schools.

• THE RELATIONSHIP MODEL OF THE JAZZ BAND CAN ALSO INFORM HOW SCHOOLS ARE ORGANIZED: The more flexible roles, the constant interplay and listening between them, the emphasis on responding to the needs of the moment and respect for improvising coherently in each new situation offers another model for the school community.

• THE NATURE OF MUSICAL ELEMENTS CAN HELP INFORM GOOD DECISION-MAKING: The experience and model of groove, rhythm, melodic counterpoint, harmony, consonance, dissonance and improvisation over chord changes can help guide decisions about school schedules, mission statements, diverse points of view and social harmony.

ACTIVITY: Look at a decision already made or about to be made and examine it from a musical point of view: Does it offer a rhythmic groove, help the teacher swing better and sing better, bring opposing views into resolution, aim for harmonic consonance, create something exciting and beautiful? If not, adjust it the way a master composer or improvisor might.

INTERLUDE III: SATISFYING ENDINGS

This section looks at various ways you can complete the musical feeling of a music class through a satisfying sense of cadence and conclusion.

Aim for Conclusion

No matter what you're practicing in the beginning and the middle of the class, it is a good idea to have a final run-through of the piece that approaches mastery. There's always something more to work on, but the goal by the end of the class is to play a piece that sounds good enough to do its work of refreshing the group. "We did it! And we sound pretty good! Not perfect yet, but pretty good!"

The Shout Out

Every minute of every class, I am watching the children and looking for their moments of noteworthy accomplishment. I sometimes end a class with "Today's Shout-out."

> "Jenny, your killer groove on the drums kept the whole piece swingin'!"

> "Mario, thanks for helping Mia with that part that was hard for her."

> "Elizabeth, that shoulder shake in our Turkish Dance was just like the real style!"

The Handshake

Just as this is a good way to make contact with each student at the beginning of each class, so does the handshake or high-five as they exit accomplish the same. Make sure they remember eye-contact!

Complete Control

Especially after vigorous movement classes and as a good way to transition to the next class, the strategy of "complete control" * works wonders. It's essentially a yoga relaxation posture, backs on the floor, arms at the side palms up and feet slightly apart and the body still.

Talk the students through tightening all the muscles in a particular body part (start with hands, arms, etc.) on the inhale and releasing them on the exhale. Give them the image of the relaxed muscles starting to feel heavy and sinking into the floor while following the breath. Each exhale helps them sink yet deeper. From here, you can talk them through an image ("a garden of beautiful flowers"), have them review the class in their mind as you talk through the activities you've done, run a string across their legs while shaking a rattle so they can practice being still in case a rattlesnake ever did the same, or telling a silly joke to see who is in such perfect complete control that they won't even laugh (I often tell them about drinking a glass of belly-button juice). At the end, gently tap them one by one to "wake up" and return to class.

Children—and adults—need this kind of quiet and calm in their lives and 30 years later, some alums still tell me how they remember these moments.

---

* Thanks to P.E. teacher Rudy Benton for both the idea and the term.

The Singing Parade

If you need to escort the children back to class, here is another opportunity to reinforce a song repertoire while going down the hall. I often do songs where you can improvise verses greeting the different people you pass—the staff at the front desk, the School Head as we pass his office, students walking down the hall the other way. It might be a song you've just done in class or one especially made for the exit.

CLOSING CIRCLE: The Takeaway

Remembering John Dewey's suggestion that we learn from reflection on experience, gather in a circle at the end of class and ask each child to name one "takeaway" from the lesson. Out of everything that happened, they have to note one thing that stood out for them. It could range from "I need to pay more attention." to "We sounded good!" The more specific the better.

> "I realized that I'm not so good at tremolo and need to work on that."

"We sounded good, but we should get softer when we repeat the first section."

Peer Appreciation

Go around the circle and ask each to appreciate a classmate for something notable they did. Typical things include:

"Great solo from Jorge!"

"Sadie really helped me out."

"I had fun making up a dance with George and Nancy. We worked really well together."

These kind of habitual reflections help build an ensemble feeling and a musical community.

The Critique

Another set of questions that helps kids think deeper about the lesson than merely doing what the teacher says:

"What did you do well? What did we as a class do well?"

"What do we need to work on?"

This can help you actually plan the next class and makes the children feel involved in their own learning, feel respected because you value their feedback.

What? So what? Now what?

Another routine that I once heard described in a talk:

1. *What did we do today?* You might write the answers up on the board or have the children write them in a journal.

2. *So what? What did it mean to you?* This could be sharing with a partner, with the whole group or writing it down.

3. *Now what? Now that you have a new skill or understanding, what do you think you're going to do with it?* This is a sophisticated question! The answer can be as simple as "Play better in the Spring Concert" but might also reach further: "Sing this song to my grandma who's in the hospital."

Visual Arts Reflection

At the end of a class, have the children express the feelings they got from the class with a drawing. (See one example in Coda)

Written Reflection

At the end of a unit, have the older children write a reflection by asking key questions. Here is a sample of an end-of-the-year evaluation form I gave my 8th graders in their jazz study (see Coda for the children's responses):

1. Someone who has never heard it asks you "What is jazz? What makes it different from other styles?" What do you say?

2. Should students in American schools study jazz? If so, why? If not, why not?
3. Should students in American schools play jazz? If so, why? What does it offer to them? If not, why not?
4. What does jazz teach us about American history?
5. What does jazz teach us about the human spirit?
6. What feeling do you get when you listen to jazz? What feeling do you get playing jazz?

SECTION II—SF School Music Program Reflection

1. What do you feel the SF School Music Program gave you over all the years?
2. What was the most memorable story in our jazz history study?
3. What was the most memorable feeling you had playing jazz this year?
4. Imagine you are grown with children of your own and they go to a school that is about to cut out the music program. You go to the school board meeting and try to convince them to keep music in the school. What do you say?

Through reflections like the above, you give the children the opportunity to answer the "so what" of their musical experience. This is a courageous step for a teacher to take! If most of the students wrote, "Your class meant nothing to me," you have some reflection yourself to do! At the other end of the spectrum, this is a chance to discover that you have made more of an impact than you ever thought you did. It is also eloquent testimony to use the next time you need to advocate for the arts.

Summary: Drawing from the above suggestions, create your own routines for endings of classes. Following musical guidelines, they can feel like a thundering cadence or slowly fade out into a welcome silence. Feel free to mix and match or use different strategies for different age levels. The important thing is to create that musical sense of satisfaction, to punctuate the sense that some worthy and occasionally wondrous journey has been travelled.

CODA

I was present at the birth of both my children and at the death of both my parents. One minute after each of my two daughters was born, I cut the umbilical cord, cradled them in my arms and welcomed them into this world. In the days before each of my parents passed, I held them in my arms and helped them let go of the cord that tethered them to life, blessing them to fly out of their mortal bodies into the next world. Music was present at both occasions, singing my loved ones into and out of this world.

In the long arc of a human life, music has been the language spoken with the kids at my school, the adults in my workshops, the elders at the Senior Center. Whether it's Bach or Bird, James Brown or Count Basie, whether I'm playing the banjo or the bagpipe, whether the music comes from Brazil or Bali, it doesn't particularly matter. It all is part of a blessed bountiful bouquet of beauty and bliss, an intricate combination of tones and rhythms that enlarges and enlivens our capacity to feel, exult and wonder.

Music became a large part of my identity, an identity that was not an inherited gift but a slowly emerging creation born of my day-to-day choices. The music I listened to and played helped shape who I became, alongside what I read, where I traveled, who I hung out with, what spiritual practices I chose. My home was at the crossroads of divergent cultures and it turned out to be a good place to live. It helped me be comfortable with opposing ways and to find the connecting roads between them. As poet Rainer Marie Rilke says:

> "Take your practiced powers and stretch them out until they
> span the chasm between contradictions ... for the god wants
> to know himself in you." *

---

* From his poem "As once the winged energy of delight."

In writing down ideas that helped guide my teaching, I started to notice the preponderance of *opposites*—repetition/variation, simple/complex, imitation/ creation, be serious/ have fun, blend in/ stand out and more. By honoring the opposites, discovering the threads that connect them, taking our "practiced powers and stretching them" to the edges of experience, the gods make themselves known. You can feel it in the unbridled joy of the children, the quality of silence in the room when the music stops, the felt presence of the unseen ancestors. We were made to hold it all.

Music can help us enter that lifelong conversation. When we hear the exquisite counterpoint in a Bach fugue, the playful polyphonies of a New Orleans brass band, the polyrhythmic patterns in a Ghanaian drum choir, we begin to understand how two lines help bring out each line more fully. We come to see that the human psyche is most alive when it is plural, not singular.

It is when we firmly plant our flag in one corner of a tiny field that the narrowing begins, that we begin to set ourselves against each other, that we punish difference, that we put to sleep all those marvelous parts of ourselves that can't live in the confined space we've chosen. True education and culture find a home for all of them and keeps them in constant conversation. The art of living is not to decide if each is needed, but rather when each is needed and how and how much. There is no rulebook or prepackaged formula for this—just a jazz musician's attention to which note is needed in the next moment.

This book is testimony to the many ways in which music can enlarge us, can rebuild that marvelous 360 degree personality we had as children before the narrowing began. Likewise, the musical teaching of music can help children claim and teachers reclaim the full measure of their intellectual, imaginative and humanitarian promise. Amidst the endless work, the low pay and status, the struggle to be given the time and space to teach to the edge of our craft, music education is worthy of the best we have to offer. Teaching music musically refreshes and uplifts us all.

The most meaningful testimony comes from the children themselves. Here is a spontaneous affirmation from Ripley, one of my 4-year old students:

Then there is the sage advice from 6-year old Amelia Lancefield Reid to all teachers. When her mother going to an Orff workshop told her that she was going to learn how to make music classes more fun, the daughter replied: "Oh, I know how to do that!" and then proceeded to outline the steps:

How to Make A Class fun for Kids

- Make There Be lots of play time
- Make there Be lots of games
- Make there Be A tiny bit of learning

Finally, the testimonies from the 8th graders at the end of their study at The San Francisco School (see Endings for the questions they answer below). We would be wise to heed their words:

Music is not just banging on a drum to make a sound. People learn history and rhythm and life skills from music. Music is a part of life because it keeps you sane, it keeps you cool and composed through the many wavy roads in what is called life.

—Josie

Music is essential to a kid's academic development. As a middle school student, the connection that I made from music to academics was astounding. I would use music techniques and to study and finish work. It was an important part of my life and I don't know where I would have been if I didn't have it.

—Sophia

Music is the key to life if taught correctly. It can open new doors and take you to places you've never been before.

—Nashira

Learning music made me think in a way I never had before. It made my brain more flexible.

—Claire

For some kids, music is the voice they never had.

—Casaun

Music is a way to work with sounds with your hands. It forms your brain, helps you to think in a different way. It's a way speak to people and a way to listen to people.

—Julianna

Without music, I would be a mess. Music is my best friend. It sticks by me through thick and thin. It makes hard times better and good times simply the best.

—Maya

Music class always put me in a happy mood. When I looked at my schedule and saw I had music, it changed my feeling about the day.

—Shalamar

Music is an alternate place for kids to exist. You might not be good at math, but could be good in music—and vice-versa. It gives a place to be creative and to learn life skills. It's a place for kids to be themselves and also bond with their classmates.

—LUCIA

As someone with a lot of personal catastrophes and trauma, music became my escape from them. I often spent my day counting minutes until I could be in music. I don't think most people realize how important the music program is to people like myself and I want more kids like myself to find their escape into music.

—JAMES

Music is what completes an education. It is such an essential part of our culture and everyday life that taking it away would be like taking away color from nature and flavor from food.

—NATE

Amen to it all. Now let's get to work.

OTHER BOOKS BY DOUG GOODKIN

ALL BLUES: Jazz for the Orff Ensemble
The first supplement to *Now's the Time,* with a special focus on the roots of the blues (13 pieces) and jazz blues (22 pieces) arranged for Orff Ensemble. CD of SF School children performing the pieces included. Pentatonic Press (2012)

INTERY MINTERY: Nursery Rhymes for Body, Voice and Orff Ensemble
48 activities for music and language arts teachers connecting music and poetry. Pentatonic Press (2008)

THE ABC's OF EDUCATION: A Primer for Schools to Come
26 ways in which schools could be refreshed. Pentatonic Press (2006)

NOW'S THE TIME: Teaching Jazz to All Ages
The groundbreaking book uniting jazz education with Orff practice. Over 60 games, speech and movement activities, Orff arrangements. Pentatonic Press (2004)

PLAY, SING AND DANCE: An Introduction to Orff Schulwerk
An overview of this dynamic approach to music education. Schott Publishers (2002)

SOUND IDEAS: Activities for Percussion Circle
Practical activities for music and classroom teachers based on Howard Gardner's Multiple Intelligences. Alfred Publications (2002)

NAME GAMES: A Collection of Musical Name Games
Practical activities that create music from your students' names. Alfred Publications (1998)

A RHYME IN TIME: Rhythm, Speech Activities and Improvisation for the Classroom
Nursery rhymes as starting point for musical exploration and improvisation in the body and voice. Alfred Publications (1997)

OTHER PENTATONIC PRESS PUBLICATIONS
FROM WIBBLETON TO WOBBLETON: Adventures in the Elements of Music and Movement—James Harding
Integrated arts lessons with graphic illustrations. Includes arrangements of nursery rhymes for Orff instruments. (2013)

BLUE IS THE SEA: Music, Dance & Visual Arts —Sofía López-Ibor
Integrated arts and activities for preschool, elementary and middle school that includes poetry, dance, drama, artwork in various media and music arranged for Orff Ensemble. Many examples of student art and photos of children, all in full vibrant color. (2011)